HONG KONG

By Robert Elegant
and the Editors of Time-Life Books

Photographs by Brian Brake

THE GREAT CITIES · TIME-LIFE BOOKS · AMSTERDAM

The Author: Robert Elegant was born in New York City in 1928. He gained his post-graduate degree in Chinese and Japanese Languages and Cultures at Columbia University in 1950, and the following year was posted to Hong Kong as Far East correspondent for the Overseas News Agency. He went to Korea as a war correspondent, later returning to Hong Kong as bureau chief for *Newsweek* magazine and later for the *Los Angeles Times*. His abiding interest in China has resulted in many books on the subject—including *China's Red Masters, The Dragon's Seed, Mao's Great Revolution* and the novel *Dynasty*. He left Hong Kong in 1976 and now lives in Ireland.

The Photographer: Brian Brake was born in Wellington, New Zealand, in 1927. He was awarded a British Council Scholarship in 1950 and subsequently joined Magnum, the photo-journalism group headed by Henri Cartier-Bresson. He has taken on assignments for leading international magazines and has exhibited his work at New York's Museum of Modern Art. He ran a documentary film company in Hong Kong until 1976, when he returned to New Zealand.

EDITOR: Dale Brown
Design Consultant: Louis Klein
Picture Editor: Pamela Marke
Assistant Picture Editor: Anne Angus

Editorial Staff for Hong Kong
Text Editors: John Cottrell, Jim Hicks
Designers: Graham Davis, Eric Molden
Staff Writers: Mike Brown, Norman Kolpas, Deborah Thompson
Picture Researcher: Jasmine Spencer
Text Researchers: Susie Dawson, Elizabeth Loving, Jackie Matthews
Design Assistants: Shirin Patel, Fiona Preston

Editorial Production for the Series
Art Department: Julia West
Editorial Department: Ellen Brush, Molly Sutherland, Betty H. Weatherley
Picture Department: Thelma Gilbert, Brigitte Guimpier, Christine Hinze

The captions and text of the picture essays were written by the staff of TIME-LIFE Books.

Valuable assistance was given in the preparation of this volume by TIME-LIFE Correspondent Bing W. Wong, Hong Kong.

Published by TIME-LIFE International (Nederland) B.V. Ottho Heldringstraat 5, Amsterdam 10 18.

ISBN 7054 0493 5

Cover: Sampans moored alongside each other create a pattern of graceful arcs in the seawall-shielded harbour at Yaumati, on the west coast of the Kowloon Peninsula.

First end paper: The swirling floral design of a Ming Dynasty lacquer box, on sale at an antique store in Hong Kong, has been created from layers of lacquer built up on the wooden base.

Last end paper: Lavishly attired images of mythological figures crowd part of an eight-foot-high paper-and-cloth tableau for the festival of Tin Hau, patron goddess of Hong Kong's fisherfolk.

TIME
LIFE
BOOKS

Contents

I

Place of Passage

The sloop *Roland Sathya* settles sweetly into the white-capped waves, fitting herself to the oily waters. Her sheets loose and sails spread to catch the following wind, she surges westwards out of Hong Kong harbour. Directly to port, in the shadow of 1,805-foot-high Victoria Peak, I can see old warehouses rimming Possession Point, where, in 1841, a British naval force first raised the Union Jack over what is today Britain's largest remaining colony. To starboard lies the quarter-of-a-mile square rock called Stonecutters Island, a 19th-Century Alcatraz.

But it is the view over the stern that draws my eyes from their proper task of watching the sails. In that direction multi-coloured apartment blocks spring from the precipitous green-and-brown hillsides, while beneath them a mile-wide strip of silver-and-green water is plied by an extra-ordinary variety of vessels—an incongruous medley of bright-varnished company launches, cargo ships of a score of nations, police and customs patrol boats, grimy motorized water-taxis called *walla-wallas*, high-pooped fishing junks, smaller sampans poled by women with babies nodding in slings on their backs, and self-important ferries dodging among the moored freighters and American warships.

The audacious natural beauty of this harbour scene overwhelms me still, even though I have viewed it a thousand times. Some partisans talk of Sydney, Naples or San Francisco, but this to me is far away the world's most spectacular city-port. It is a landfall made all the more dramatic because Hong Kong's New York-style skyline rises steeply on either side of a strait varying in width from one to six miles. The two sides of the densely packed metropolis—hemmed in by their backdrops of hills—are joined by a mile-long underwater road tunnel, the longest in Asia.

The northern side is called Kowloon (Nine Dragons) because it was built on nine hills at the tip of a minuscule peninsula jutting out from the south-east mainland of China. It occupies only 3.25 square miles, but immediately to its north (starting at Boundary Street) lie the New Territories, 370.5 square miles of mountainous land that the Colony of Hong Kong holds on a 99-year lease from China. On the opposite side of the harbour is Victoria (originally named Queen's Town), an intensely developed administrative and commercial centre clinging to the northern shore of Hong Kong Island. The island's rumpled topography assures that Victoria's "satellite" communities, like the port of Aberdeen on the south side, enjoy an insularity of their own, while remaining within easy driving distance of the metropolitan area.

A Jumbo jetliner swoops over Victoria Harbour and the high-rise apartment buildings of Kowloon on its approach to Hong Kong's Kai Tak Airport. Hong Kong's intercourse with the outside world is conducted almost entirely by air or sea: a single railway connects the Colony to the People's Republic.

Beyond the dividing strait, to the east and the west, the Colony also has 235 islands, mostly too small or too barren for habitation. They are strewn like mottled jade carvings on the silky surface of the South China Sea, but not one can compare with this view of Hong Kong. No human habitation, I say to myself, has the right to be so unabashedly gorgeous.

Yet so much more than its location makes Hong Kong breathtaking. Almost half of its four-and-half million inhabitants have come from elsewhere seeking economic or political freedom, and many do not consider themselves permanent residents—with good reason. Hong Kong is the only major metropolis with a built-in time-fuse, a self-destruct mechanism set to explode in 1997 when the lease of the ceded New Territories expires and nine-tenths of the Colony reverts to China. In this unique city-port, East and West are intermixed to an unrivalled degree; here, two disparate ideologies co-exist in a burgeoning cosmopolis that combines the magic and mystery and colour of the Orient with the wonders of the technological age. It is, at one and the same time, the city of Suzy Wong and supersonic jets, of sampans and hydrofoils, fortune-tellers and fortune-hunters.

That there is a Hong Kong at all is a miracle. There are 404 square miles of land in the Colony, but because of the hills and mountains 80 per cent of it is not suitable for either farming or building. There are hardly any natural resources, not even sufficient food and water. Only dogged perseverance could enable four-and-a-half million persons to live and prosper here. Their greatest achievement has been the transformation of Hong Kong from a vast shopping centre—probably the biggest and most garish in the world, selling primarily other people's goods—into a booming manufacturing complex.

A century-and-a-half ago Hong Kong was no more than a sleepy harbour: "Fragrant Harbour" as the Chinese called it—a part of the Chinese province of Kwangtung. But Royal Navy Captain Charles Elliot, Great Britain's Superintendent of Trade for China, saw its potential and had the foresight to choose Hong Kong as the British commercial and naval base when the Chinese were pressed to cede land to Britain at the close of the Opium War of 1839-42. (Kowloon and Stonecutters Island were ceded in 1860 after another armed confrontation between the British and the Chinese.) Elliot's sound judgment earned him the sack. Lord Palmerston, then British Foreign Secretary, censured Elliot for his stupidity in allowing the Manchu government to fob off "a barren island with hardly a house upon it". Young Queen Victoria, just four years on the throne, recorded how husband Albert was "so much amused" by this utterly trivial addition to her overseas possessions.

It was a natural enough reaction, I suppose. Why should anyone in London, 7,852 miles away, be impressed by the addition to the vast British Empire of 29 square miles of irregularly shaped rock, 10 miles in length and varying from two to five miles in width? At that time the island

All his possessions packed into canvas bags, an emigrant at Kai Tak Airport awaits the call for his flight to West Germany. More than 45,000 Chinese leave Hong Kong annually, mostly destined for Western countries; in turn a nearly equal number of people arrive in the metropolis each year from mainland China.

was primarily a haven for pirates and opium smugglers, and it had fewer than 6,000 inhabitants. The rock was virtually devoid of agricultural land and of level areas on which to erect dwellings. Moreover, it lacked sufficient drinking water to support a population of more than a few tens of thousands. And even when typhoons delivered desperately needed additional water into the reservoirs, there was, of course, a heavy price to pay in terms of death and destruction. With the exception of three months of the year, the climate was either drenchingly hot and humid or dankly cold. Worst of all, malaria was endemic and cholera, typhoid and bubonic plague regularly visited the poor fishermen who lived there.

Today the climate is the same, with typhoons still roaring out of the South China Sea on freak days between June and September; but disease has been conquered, level areas for housing have been created by land reclamation projects, and gigantic new reservoirs have been constructed to provide adequate drinking water. More than a million people now live on Palmerston's "barren island", and another 2.4 million cram Kowloon—a noisy hive of toiling workers and pleasure-peddling touts that bursts with shops, bars, brothels, clubs, factories, skyscrapers and shabby tenements festooned with laundry. Sections of Kowloon have the dubious distinction of being among the most densely populated areas in the world, with more than 388,000 inhabitants per square mile.

While Kowloon barely offers room to breathe and Victoria is almost as claustrophobic, there are still places in the Colony—thanks to the limitations placed on human settlement by the mountains and hills—where it is possible to get away from the din and crowds. Hong Kong Island itself has a few exquisite bays and peaceful rural walks to offer, but true country—and an older China—can be found on some of the adjacent islands and, most especially, in the New Territories. And then of course there are the ubiquitous waters on which I have spent so many hours relaxing aboard *Roland*, washing away the cares of a cosmopolis that at times can seem absolutely mad.

This sometimes nerve-racking, often enchanting, but always invigorating Crown Colony has been my home for more than a quarter of a century. I am what is known as a "Hong Kong belonger", a registered resident of this realm for refugees and transients. But now career interests impel me to leave, and before bidding Hong Kong farewell, I am taking a last cruise. My emotions are as roiled as the choppy waters through which *Roland* sails. Regrets assail me on all sides. I continue to be both fascinated and repelled by the sweeping changes that 25 years have wrought upon Victoria and Kowloon and the surrounding areas. A chief occupation of Hong Kong is destroying old structures and replacing them with higher and more functional buildings, meanwhile spreading macadam tentacles of roads ever farther into the steep, green hills.

With its distinctive sails close-hauled in a light breeze, a junk heads into Hong Kong harbour with cargo from China. Still the workhorse of traders and fishermen of the China Seas, the junk has hardly changed its appearance in more than a thousand years, although nowadays it is often motorized.

Clear of Victoria Harbour, I can see where the old *S.S. Queen Elizabeth*, destroyed by fire in 1972, lay for years while workmen picked her apart, swarming over her immensity like industrious ants dismembering an enormous caterpillar. When gargantuan American aircraft-carriers call at Hong Kong, they anchor in this area. The inner harbour of Hong Kong is too shallow for their great bulk.

I bring in the sheets and *Roland* reaches southwards into the channel formed by Hong Kong Island's western coast and Lamma Island. Dominated by 1,147-foot Mount Stenhouse, Lamma is one of the few places in the Colony where the categorical imperative of industrial expansion has been rejected: public protest prevented the construction of an oil refinery there. Today most of Lamma's 3,000 inhabitants still fish for a living.

The East Lamma Channel is overcast, obscured in part by the black smoke drifting from the high stacks of the electric power-generating plant on the tip of Ap Lei Chau (Duck's Tongue Island), an islet on my port side that shelters busy Aberdeen Harbour. Here the big, seagoing fishing junks are tied up in noisome, filth-encrusted waters beside gaudily painted floating restaurants that are the tourists' delight and the despair of environmentalists who fret over the garbage they disgorge.

My mahogany-hulled sloop passes round Ap Lei Chau and soon, on my left, I can see Deep Water Bay and Repulse Bay glittering in the cold, brilliant winter sunshine. Above the green waters the hills are thick with high-rises, and an 18-storey white slab rears over the old, extravagantly gracious Repulse Bay Hotel. I remember when only two low blocks of flats were tucked among the hills above the sandy beach, and older Hong Kong inhabitants can recall when Repulse Bay was a quiet summer resort for the well-to-do Europeans who came south from Victoria, crossing the island's hill spine in their pony traps to consume enormous curry tiffins in the splendid hotel. Repulse Bay is no longer a secluded retreat. In 1975 some disused buildings were transformed into a complex of restaurants, ranging from a franchised hamburger stand to a superb seafood house. Shopping centres and a highly fashionable residential area have further transformed it into a concrete Riviera for Europeans and Americans drawn to Hong Kong by the lure of quick profits.

Neighbouring Deep Water Bay, once a peaceful haven too, is today clamorous with the outboard motors of its water-skiing club, only one of its several "improvements". Fortunately, *Roland's* distance from the shore obscures the off-putting details of the two bays. New angular structures, assertive in their numbers, merge and partly efface themselves. Since even the ceaseless burrowing and building of industrious Chinese workmen have not totally altered the fundamental contours of the land, the effect is pleasantly misleading, the overall impression startlingly bucolic.

Sails bellying, *Roland* reaches farther south-east, towards the jutting promontory called Stanley where the enormous twin steel-tracery cups of a

Midday shoppers—combing the stalls for fresh food, off-the-peg clothes and cheap goods— swarm the length of a street market in Victoria. Open-air marts, an integral part of Chinese life, are found in all the communities that make up the Hong Kong conurbation.

communications satellite earth-station rise from the green hills like surrealistic white mushrooms. One antenna is cocked east against the cloud-hung sky to receive and transmit across the broad reaches of the Pacific Ocean. The other antenna points westwards towards the fragrant, indolent lands of South-East Asia, the turmoil of the Indian subcontinent and the oil-sands of the Middle East.

I prefer not to draw too close to Stanley, which the Chinese, stubbornly clinging to old names, call Red Pillars, presumably because of the russet colour of the headland soil. It holds for me too many joyous memories. Eastwards, just across the narrow neck of the promontory, is Tai Tam village and the minute house that my family and I occupied for two years. When we moved into that house in 1957, Stanley itself was primarily a fishing community, although it was dominated by the Lai Cheung brewery, producer of pungent Chinese rice-wine which, in spite of its name, is a sort of non-fizzy beer. Now, soaring blocks of flats have mushroomed in the area, and the four-room house we rented for $84 (United States) a month fetches at least five times that amount—still comparatively cheap when the rent for many commonplace flats in Hong Kong is as much as $2,500 a month. (Although the Colony has its own currency, the Hong Kong dollar, I shall express all sums in this book in U.S. dollars for easier understanding.)

In 1959 I was offered the leasehold of that little house standing on less than a tenth of an acre for $8,000. About 15 years later its estimated worth was at least $80,000! Thus does inflation and, more important, Hong Kong's relentless growth make all except the most canny residents regret lost economic opportunities. But my own regrets this day are not financial, although I might bemoan the fact that, unlike many others, I have not grown rich here.

I was originally drawn to Hong Kong in 1951 not by a dream of wealth, but by the romantic lure of Asia and by the Colony's proximity to China. Hong Kong richly fulfilled its promise to open new political and intellectual frontiers to me and to serve as a base for adventures throughout Asia as an American news-magazine correspondent. Moreover, its people were generous in their affection and their tutelage—but then I was lucky to have the stubborn persistence and enough command of the Chinese language to penetrate behind their sometimes abrasive exteriors.

Ah Yick, a burly Cantonese with bristling black hair, found us that house in Tai Tam village when it was still a shell gutted by a typhoon that swept out of the South China Sea in the summer of 1957. Ah Yick has been dead these many years. When he flourished as Stanley's unofficial town crier and mayor, his general store served a community hardly larger than a small village—a few dozen foreigners, if one does not count the British troops stationed at Stanley Fort, and perhaps a thousand or so Chinese, mostly fishermen. It was quite isolated, some 14 miles over the narrow roads that wind through hills and along the precipices to Victoria, a long way in a cosmopolis as compact as Hong Kong.

Ah Yick, I remember, sold me a bottle of Chateau Lafite-Rothschild for $1.50 because he wanted to clear out old stock. My wife and I savoured the velvety wine and, since we were young and naïve, saved half the bottle for the next day. When we sipped the remaining wine, it had undergone a revolting transformation into rough Beaujolais. Our cook volunteered cheerfully that he had brought about the transformation to save us money; needing a large bottle to hold soya-sauce, he thought better of buying one and emptied a half-bottle of Beaujolais into the Lafite-Rothschild.

The small house precisely suited us after alterations by the ingenious master-builder, M. K. Law; my work was exciting; our friends were stimulating; my Volkswagen convertible was ideal for the island; and the junk I then sailed was both fast and comfortable. I have changed within myself since those days; dissatisfaction is, after all, a human trait. Besides, Hong Kong's arrogant display of great wealth, amid millions who toil simply to survive, breeds contentment in neither those who possess that wealth nor the less fortunate.

Although Stanley still looks like a Chinese village, more than a thousand foreigners now live in flats in the area and the Chinese population has increased several fold. Materially, life is much more convenient and comfortable. TV aerials sprout from the little houses and all the fishing junks are powered by diesel engines. A supermarket has opened, and Ah Yick's Store, itself greatly enlarged, now stocks food unobtainable in the 1950s. But no one will ever again buy Lafite-Rothschild—or even Beaujolais—for $1.50. Adolescent British soldiers still drink themselves sodden on beer in shops fronting on the footpath that meanders through Stanley Market. The market, however, has become a hectic shopping centre for both foreigners and Chinese, attracted by cheap handicrafts from the People's Republic. Fishermen still peddle fresh-caught shrimps and crabs in open pails, but a few yards away an art gallery offers works of imagination that far transcend the routine tourist trade paintings of coolies and junks with sails aglow against the purple dusk.

Behind its refurbished façade Stanley clings to its old ways. Along the foreshore of Stanley Bay, just a few hundred yards from new blocks of flats, a fishing and farming village functions as it did 20 or 50 or even a hundred years ago. Children continue to practise laboriously the intricate Chinese ideographs on squared paper; and the great Chinese festivals go on here as they always have with feasts and presentations of Cantonese operas financed by the Kaifong associations, the local community councils, whose name literally means "neighbourhood societies".

On my last visit to Stanley they were celebrating the feast-day of *Kuan Yin*, the Goddess of Mercy. Women bore offerings to her temple. Near by, a great tent seating 500 had been erected for a five-hour operatic perform-

A Titanic Trading Post

Spilling from the south-eastern border of China into the South China Sea (inset map, right), the cove-scalloped peninsulas and islands of Hong Kong (inset map, below) subsume a land area of 404 square miles. The modern city (main map) centres around Victoria Harbour, where British traders established their base in the 19th Century. On the harbour side of Hong Kong Island are government offices, business headquarters, and entertainment dens. North of the harbour, apartment blocks and factories pack Kowloon Peninsula, and Kai Tak Airport thrusts a two-mile runway into Kowloon Bay.

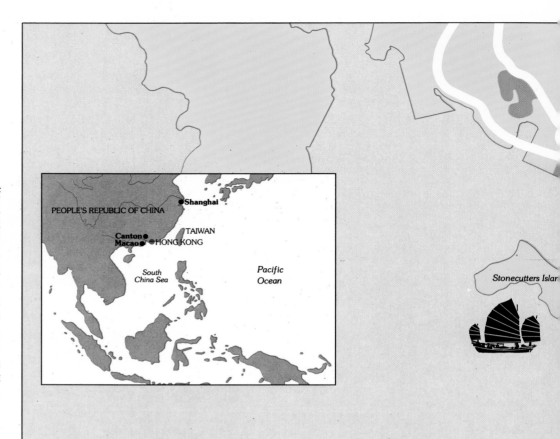

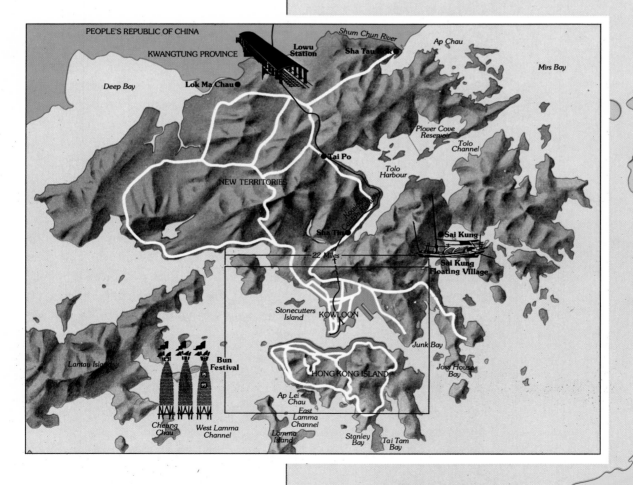

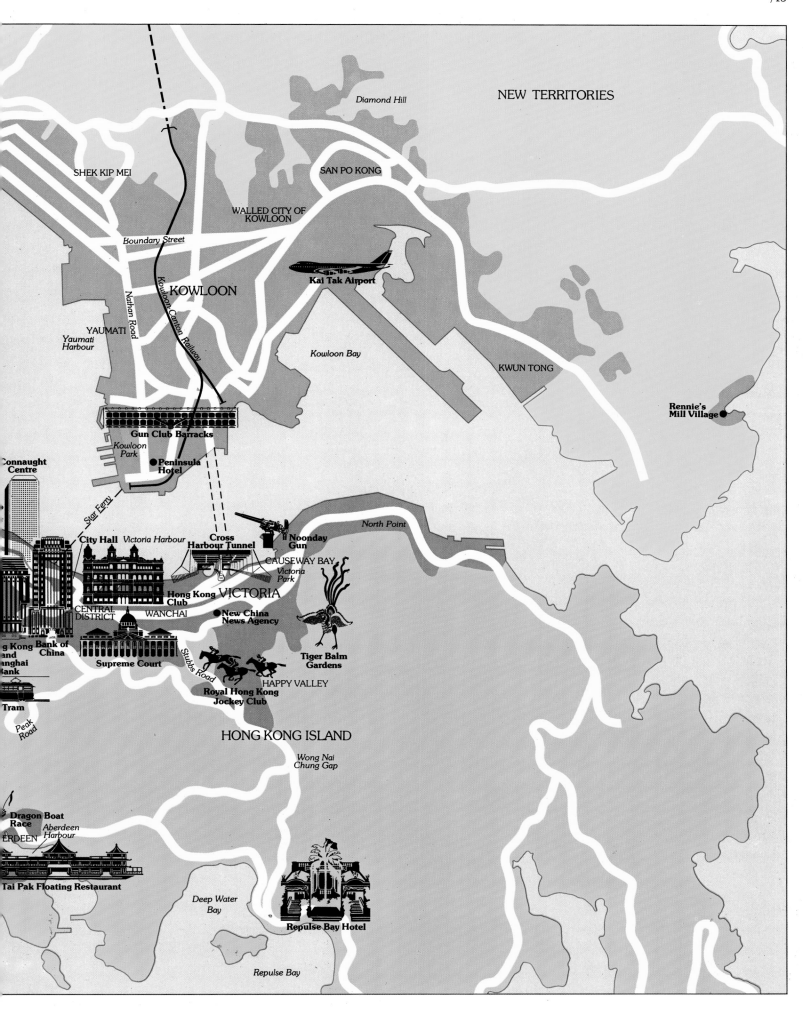

NEW TERRITORIES

Diamond Hill

SHEK KIP MEI

SAN PO KONG

WALLED CITY OF
KOWLOON

Boundary Street

KOWLOON

Kai Tak Airport

YAUMATI

*Yaumati
Harbour*

Kowloon Bay

KWUN TONG

**Rennie's
Mill Village**

Gun Club Barracks

*Kowloon
Park*

● **Peninsula
Hotel**

**Connaught
Centre**

North Point

City Hall *Victoria Harbour*

**Cross
Harbour Tunnel**

● **Noonday
Gun**

CAUSEWAY BAY

*Victoria
Park*

**Hong Kong
Club** VICTORIA

CENTRAL
DISTRICT WANCHAI

● **New China
News Agency**

**Bank of
China**

Supreme Court

Stubbs Road

HAPPY VALLEY

**Tiger Balm
Gardens**

g Kong
and
anghai
ank

Tram

**Royal Hong Kong
Jockey Club**

*Peak
Road*

HONG KONG ISLAND

*Wong Nai
Chung Gap*

**Dragon Boat
Race**

*Aberdeen
Harbour*

RDEEN

Tai Pak Floating Restaurant

*Deep Water
Bay*

Repulse Bay Hotel

Repulse Bay

ance by heavily painted players costumed in the gaudy silks of kings, mandarins, generals and ladies of the imperial court. On another occasion I attended the birthday celebration of the deity Tin Hau, the Motherly Empress of Heaven. Since she is the patroness deity of fishermen, her feast-day is the most important of Stanley's festivals, marked by processions of fishermen who wind through the streets flaunting banners, clashing cymbals and setting off firecrackers. But I have digressed—swept along as I have been by my memories.

It is late afternoon, and so I bring *Roland* about on a course around Lamma Island back to Victoria. *Roland* carries me close to Cheung Chau (Long Island). Looming behind it, to the north-west, is Lantau (Rocky Mount), the Colony's largest island, almost double the size of Hong Kong Island. Lantau was practically without inhabitants until 1951, when a community of Trappist monks, many of them refugees from mainland China, settled there and began attacking the steep hillsides and carving out level fields to grow rice and barley. For years Lantau was ideal for picnics. But in the 1970s, it too fell victim to intensive development. It is now fringed with flossy resort hotels.

Cheung Chau has fared much better. It is still largely untouched by Hong Kong's compulsive growth, being too small to invite agricultural development or to interest entrepreneurs. Its life centres on its fishing fleet, supplier of the sea-food its noisy, informal restaurants serve. There are few motor vehicles to clog its narrow streets and its people are free of the tension that makes most of Hong Kong so stimulating and—at the same time—so irritating.

In May, Cheung Chau is the scene of the *Ta Chiu* (Spirit-placating Festival) which lasts four days and nights and ends with a raucous climax called the Bun Festival. During those four days the islanders eschew meat and seafood in respect for the departed souls of fish and animals. Then, on the fourth night, the community gathers around three bun "mountains": 60-foot-high bamboo scaffoldings studded with buns and resembling a trio of moon-rockets poised for lift-off (*pages 124-5*). At a signal, scores of local lads scramble up the "mountains" in a race for the top-most buns that guarantee good fortune. Hoping that the good luck will rub off, everyone consumes at least one of the remaining buns before the night's end. Such festivals are by no means limited to Hong Kong's backwaters. Scores occur in Victoria and Kowloon every year, and provide a measure of gaiety that goes a long way to leaven the lives of Hong Kong's hard-working people. They fulfil a deeper purpose as well; they help keep the inhabitants in touch with their ancient roots.

Beneath their brisk, materialistic exteriors, the international financier and his clerks, the multi-millionaire factory-owner and his workers are bound alike, not only by the ties of family, but by universal superstition.

They see nothing odd in resorting to astrologers and fortune-tellers for guidance in their daily endeavours. Unceasing effort is expended on attempts to discern the will of Heaven and to manipulate fate for man's benefit. The *feng shui* man (literally the words mean "wind and water"), a kind of geomancer who "reads" those elements, advises his clients on how best to propitiate evil spirits and to please benevolent ones by correctly siting houses and ancestors' graves, and even by re-arranging furniture.

Confidence in their ability to manipulate fate has made Hong Kong's Chinese a race of dedicated gamblers. This avid pursuit of easy wealth is facilitated by the Portuguese overseas province of Macao, the oldest European settlement in the Far East, lying 40 miles to the west. Five square miles in size and only an hour by hydrofoil from Victoria, Macao lives by its casinos, its one-armed bandits, its jai-alai stadium and its Canidrome, where lean greyhounds race.

In Hong Kong itself, the inhabitants' readiness for a flutter—a single bet of $100,000 is only mildly sensational—is indirectly responsible for a range of social services. Consider the Royal Hong Kong Jockey Club. Some cynical observers contend that the club, rather than His Excellency the Governor, really rules the Colony, and it is easy to see why. The Jockey Club, a non-profit establishment with 7,000 members, controls all horse-racing, the only form of organized gambling (besides government lotteries, which are also controlled by the Jockey Club) that is legal in the Colony.

The Jockey Club has two race courses strategically located in Hong Kong and each year makes tens of millions of dollars from on-course and off-course betting. Some of the profits are ploughed back into improving racing facilities and the rest goes to charity—including, on average, $8 million a year given to construction costs of religious, medical and educational buildings. Many more millions have, ever since 1917, financed public amenities and eleemosynary activities too numerous to mention. As one old hand explains: "The best—if not the only—possible way to get money for charity from Hong Kong Chinese is through gambling." Moreover, through a betting tax and income from lotteries the government gets well over $25 million a year. The efficiency and effectiveness of the operation cannot be denied.

As dusk descends, *Roland* slips into the harbour on the dying breeze, making a long tack towards the tip of Kowloon peninsula. The water reflects the restless shimmer of the polychrome lights of Nathan Road, the main thoroughfare that bisects the length of Kowloon. It stretches for some two miles, from the monumental Peninsula Hotel on the waterfront to Boundary Street in the north, where the New Territories begin. The towering advertising signs that fringe the harbour assert the names of European, American and Japanese industry. For newcomers to Hong Kong this is the magic moment—when the glowing neon and the lights on ships and sampans transform the harbour into an illuminated wonderland and the streets begin to pulse with night-time activity.

As I gaze out on the sparkling scene, I realize that yet another of the things that makes Hong Kong so exciting is its compactness. Nothing is very far from anything else. Repulse Bay on the south side of Hong Kong Island is but a 15-minute drive from the bar-and-brothel district of Wanchai on the north side, and what a contrast there is between the two! Sin and corruption are big business in Wanchai. Here are the massage parlours, topless nightclubs, secret society hide-outs and drug-pushers whose paradoxical sense of fair-dealing regularly kills unwitting foreign clientele by providing them with heroin 10 times purer than the product they normally buy. Wanchai, not surprisingly, has been a gold-mine for corrupt officers of the Royal Hong Kong Police Force, some of whom have accumulated fortunes of several million dollars from graft.

In the old city of Victoria, winding alleys and steep ladder streets (flights of steps flanked by shops) persist a hundred yards from the expressways that now girdle the island. On the steep hillsides, mock Ming Dynasty palaces with blue-and-green tiled roofs perch beside Spanish villas. Higher still, following the contours of the hills, lines of weathered grey squatters' huts look down on the hanging gardens and terraced villas.

The people of Hong Kong—jammed into the available living space—are as multifarious as their dwellings. More than 98 per cent of the population can be described as Chinese on the basis of language or place of origin. But that loose definition embraces people of diverse racial origins, prejudices and customs: Chiu-chows from the mainland coastal city of Swatow, who almost monopolize the wholesale drug traffic; Mongols yearning for their broad, flat steppes; Tibetans remembering their snow-covered mountains; Chinese Muslims who virtuously avoid pork for their own delicious mutton dishes; green-eyed traders from Chinese Turkestan; and big-boned, slow-spoken refugees still nostalgic for their former lives in Shantung and Peking.

And no survey of Hong Kong's Chinese would be complete without the Colony's most picturesque community: the 79,000 boat people, chiefly Tanka and Hoklo, members of minority groups of obscure origin who have lived for centuries on the waters of southern China. Many of these fisher-folk spend their whole lives on junks. But this floating population has been fast declining, partly because the motorization of junks has reduced the size of crews required. Recently tens of thousands of boat people have moved ashore to take jobs in industry, while some Tanka (wanderers by nature) have become waiters in Chinese restaurants abroad.

Although their numbers have never been precisely established, the Cantonese undoubtedly make up the largest section of the Chinese population. The first migrants to Hong Kong—people called Punti (local inhabitants)—came from the Canton region in the 14th Century. They

Hedged in by high-rise apartment houses, the Po Kok Buddhist Temple and School for Girls in Happy Valley, on Hong Kong Island, has managed to retain its own oasis of greenery. Pagoda-style roofs of the sort on the buildings belonging to this complex are fast becoming a rarity in the metropolis.

were to be followed by the Hakka (guest people), a peasant group who now make up the biggest Cantonese section and who are as dedicated to the land as the orthodox Tankas and Hoklos are wedded to the sea.

Aside from the Cantonese, the most obtrusive of all Chinese in the Hong Kong melting pot are the quick-witted Shanghailanders who have created their own "Shanghai moved south" at North Point, on the island's north coast. The sizzling dialect of the former commercial capital of China is heard here more often than staccato Cantonese; sybaritic Shanghai bath-houses refresh the body and the spirit; and restaurants and food shops offering that city's eclectic cuisine take care of the appetite.

The non-Chinese community numbers about 70,000. Scattered throughout the Colony like raisins in the saffron rice of a *buryani* are Indians of a dozen different tribes, castes and regions—among them Sindhis and Mawaris who are successful merchants, and Pathans, Sikhs and Punjabis who serve as professional guards and watchmen. The British predominate among the Europeans. But Hong Kong has attracted representatives of almost every European country and many Americans and Australians as well. The Jewish community, numbering no more than 500, includes multi-millionaires of Iraqi origin, refugees from Hitler's Germany, fugitive families from Lenin's (not Stalin's) Soviet Union who escaped via Shanghai, and one or two families who have been associated with Hong Kong almost since the beginning. But the majority of the non-Chinese are temporary residents—although some stay for decades. And out of liaisons and marriages between foreigners and Chinese have come the Eurasians, thousands of them, forming a vital, close-meshed community of their own.

Hong Kong Chinese lead intensely public lives. Courtship and marriage, illness and death, worship and quarrels, almost the acts of procreation and birth, it sometimes seems, all take place in the crowded streets of Hong Kong. Ancient and new China can be seen at every turn: old men in long gowns airing their pet birds or crickets in bamboo cages and devoted Maoist cadres in high-collared tunics; girls in sexy skirts and elderly ladies with bound feet; hard-working coolies in black pyjamas and young toughs in blue jeans. The variety is indescribable. For China is not a nation but a continent—and Hong Kong is China at her most vigorously uninhibited.

My sentimental voyage ends at the Royal Hong Kong Yacht Club in Causeway Bay. When I first knew it, the club stood grandly aloof on an islet connected to Hong Kong Island by a causeway. Now it is encysted by progress, its once spacious anchorage half-filled by the unending reclamation that over the years has extended the foreshore for several hundred yards on a 2.5 mile front. The web of concrete expressways that prevents total coagulation of traffic (some 200,000 vehicles on 650 miles of road) has encroached upon the club's privacy, as have the approaches to the cross-harbour tunnel.

A large, crownless hat trimmed with a black valance identifies this elderly lady, taking a midday rest, as a member of the Hakka segment of Hong Kong's Chinese population. Originally from North China, the Hakka settled in the New Territories during the 16th Century and won an enduring reputation for hard work and deep allegiance to their own customs.

All the same, the Yacht Club has fared better than the Cricket Club, formerly the most familiar symbol of British Colonial rule and Chinese Communist toleration. Photographers could never resist the ironic contrast: white-flannelled Englishmen playing cricket among the skyscrapers of the world's most expensive real estate, against a backdrop of the Communist Bank of China adorned by a five-storey-high portrait of Chairman Mao and clouds of red bunting. Now the Cricket Club, compelled after 124 years to make way for a public park, has been shifted to a location in Wong Nai Chung Gap on the road to Repulse Bay. In its new location it has become a luxurious and expensive refuge, complete with saunas, swimming pool, and tennis and squash courts. It did not boast such splendours in its salad days in downtown Victoria. Then it served chiefly not only the *taipans* (Great Managers) of the big companies that run Hong Kong, but provided their juniors with cheap lunches, opportunities for exercise and a convenient after-work bar. (This last facility was almost excessive; no more than Dublin does Hong Kong lack places to drink.)

The government's hypersensitivity to constantly repeated accusations that it favours the wealthy and the "expatriates", Hong Kong's idiosyncratic term for non-Chinese residents, lay behind the Cricket Club removal. Even so, it is not certain that the new public park on the club's old site will survive. Like many other fripperies it may finally be engorged by the business district, which is rapidly expanding from the narrow canyon of Queen's Road Central, the original High Street of Victoria, eastwards towards the Yacht Club. The original plexus of Hong Kong, called simply "Central" by both the Chinese-speaking and English-speaking residents, has itself been wholly altered in recent years. Old Hong Kong has almost disappeared and the assertive symbol of the new is the 52-storey, dominolike Connaught Centre, an office block whose circular windows make inevitable the polite nickname "The Swiss Cheese" (*page 193*), and the much less polite nickname, here bowdlerized, "The House of Ten Thousand Orifices".

When I first came to the Colony in 1951, Kai Tak Airport on the Kowloon side, had not yet been extended far out into the harbour to make a dramatic, 11,130-foot-long landing strip (*pages 188-9*). The view I had as I crossed to Victoria on the Star Ferry was virtually indistinguishable from the vista that in 1900 greeted arrivals on the steamers of the Peninsular and Oriental Line, better known as the P. & O. Now, alas, the low, crenellated buildings, with canopied arcades that sheltered pedestrians from the fierce sun, have given way to singularly unimaginative, yet collectively breathtaking slabs of glass, concrete and steel. Gone, too, is the wooden Star Ferry Pier of western Victoria with its clock tower resembling the steeple of a village church, so well-suited to the village Hong Kong then was. In its place stands a low, concrete terminus four times the size of the original, capped by a dwarfish clock-tower that suggests a dunce's cap.

With ground space at a premium, rooftops serve as exercise yards for the 400 racehorses kept at the high-rise stables of the Royal Hong Kong Jockey Club.

Even the new doesn't last long in this city of constant change. The Alexandra House, an office tower completed in 1956, was torn down in the mid-1970s to make way for a still higher Alexandra House that can hardly be distinguished from its neighbours. More lamentably, the General Post Office, built in 1913 of red brick adorned with green cupolas, and one of the last survivors of those gracious, unhurried days, has also been razed.

Among the few buildings of the past to remain is the last citadel of old Colonial architecture and old Colonial privilege: the wedding-cake Hong Kong Club, next to the Cenotaph on Club Street in Victoria. To all Hong Kong, the white, four-storey building embellished with bright blue cornices is still The Club, its membership, in theory at least, limited to the "number ones" and "number twos" of established companies. If the Hong Kong Club is also swept aside, the Colony will have completed the process of altering its face and its psychology profoundly.

I chose not to join The Club in the days when Chinese were barred from membership, but now I catch myself hoping that the demise of this last bastion of privilege will be long delayed. Thus does sentiment—and, confessedly, the excellence of the food offered in its red-damask-hung dining-room—make compromisers of us all. However, even my sentimentality will not allow me to accept The Club ritual of after-dinner coffee served by a rotund black waiter attired in a costume suitable for a Nubian slave or a Turkish eunuch, complete with a red-velvet waistcoat.

Taking a final look from *Roland's* deck, it occurs to me that only one man-made feature of the panorama remains unchanged from long ago: the Kowloon-Canton Railway, completed in 1912 and still running to China, in spite of the intermittent troubles and breakdowns in East-West relations. The terminus has been shifted eastwards from its old red brick building near the Peninsula Hotel to a cheaper location in drab concrete structures where land will be more readily available for expansion. But the railway itself is still visible from the sea, a shining steel umbilical cord to Mother China stretching across the hills of the New Territories, along the shore of island-dotted Tolo Harbour from Sha Tin (Sandy Fields) to Tai Po (Big Causeway), then inland through the mountain valleys to the border that is 17 miles long and roughly marked by the Shum Chun (Deep River). The railway carries both freight and passengers from assertively bourgeois, self-indulgent Hong Kong to socialist, self-consciously austere China. Passengers alight to cross the wooden bridge (*pages 158-9*) over Shum Chun on foot and board other cars on the Communist side. The Communists do not permit foreign carriages to enter their territory.

"Legal entrants" to Hong Kong—Chinese who have obtained coveted exit visas from the Communist authorities—walk across the bridge that links two completely different worlds. Although fearful of the unknown, most are elated at finally emerging from the Motherland they have chosen to leave forever. "Illegal entrants", those unable to obtain visas, occasionally dare the heavily guarded land frontier, but the majority—incalculable thousands *every year*—choose to swim to a less trammelled life. By night, supported by inflated pigs' bladders, blown-up trousers tied at the cuffs, or other makeshift waterwings, they cross shark-menaced Mirs Bay or much patrolled Deep Bay.

By 1974 legal and illegal immigration, then totalling 50,000 to 60,000 a year, was putting severe strain on Hong Kong's housing and social services. The government became so alarmed that it declared it would return illegal entrants who were apprehended, unless humanitarian considerations dictated otherwise. In practice, however, the procedure has not changed significantly since the 1949 Revolution prompted refugees to begin stealing across the land and sea frontiers. It is estimated that only one-third of all illegal immigrants are detected, and only a small minority are sent back to China. The vast majority remain in the Colony. Some lie low indefinitely. Others are allowed by the basically sympathetic authorities to register as Hong Kong "belongers" and are given blue plastic identity cards —legal passports to the new but uncertain way of life for which they yearn.

Tomorrow my wife and I take off from Kai Tak Airport. Most "belongers" it seems, plan for the day when they depart from this place of passage; we did too. Yet, now that the day is at hand I am struck by surpassing sadness. It has been so easy, so obvious to look back down the years and note how Hong Kong has changed—so often for the worse. But as Samuel Johnson observed, the prospect of hanging concentrates a man's mind wonderfully. My eyes sharpened by awareness of imminent departure and prolonged absence, I now see Hong Kong's undiminished attractions—all the things that I now take for granted, including the heroic quality of its people.

The history of Hong Kong is not an idyll. The island was torn ignominiously from the Chinese Empire to serve Britain as a base for opium-smuggling. It has made no spectacular contribution to the well-being or the exaltation of mankind, unless the isolation of the organism that causes the Black Death, *bacillus pasturella pestis* (by Japanese medical men working in Hong Kong during the Colony's Great Plague of 1894) can be considered such a contribution. Its annals are besmirched by bloodshed, callousness, greed, cruelty and corruption. Nonetheless, the story of Hong Kong unfolds as an extraordinary epic of survival; and, above all, as a classic record of human adaptability.

Modern Jewel in a Timeless Setting

A tubby, white Kowloon ferry approaches the Victoria waterfront, where skyscrapers glow in stormy light beneath the shrouded hump of Victoria Peak.

Rich, artificial, glitteringly modern, a concentrated patch of capitalist enterprise humming with urban intensity, Hong Kong hangs to a largely rural edge of Communist China like a single jigsaw fragment from an unrelated picture. The crowded concrete-and-glass skyscrapers of Victoria and Kowloon, facing each other across the narrow, busy harbour, stun visitors with a dramatic first impression. But a wider view soon brings into focus other aspects of Hong Kong's visual character: the populous fishing port of Aberdeen; green, sparsely inhabited outer islands; a maze of coves and inlets lapped by the South China Sea. Even where man-made Hong Kong dazzles most, such as Victoria (above), it cannot overpower the precipitous hills looming beyond—the old natural land shapes that are an essential part of the beauty of this gem of a metropolis.

In the subtropical night, the glimmering lights of Kowloon (at top) and Victoria (foreground) wrap a garland around the dark mirror of the harbour.

At Aberdeen, on the south side of Hong Kong Island, modern housing projects overlook a "floating village" of junks in the harbour behind the islet.

Its hills crowded with small farms, the narrow-necked island of Cheung Chau lies within Hong Kong waters, 12 miles from crowded Hong Kong Island.

Only scattered signs of human presence intrude upon these islands and hills of the northern New Territories, sharply etched against the graded blues of the sea.

2

The Lion and the Dragon

The view westwards from the tenth floor of the Hong Kong Hilton is hedged by the narrow canyon of Queen's Road Central. It offers no more than a circumscribed glimpse of a concrete and glass-lined business street that might be seen from any window in any metropolis, or so it appears at a glance. But for me the view encapsulates the past, present and future of Hong Kong. It takes in two buildings, side by side, that symbolize the chief forces whose constant, often abrasive interaction created this Crown Colony, shaped its character, still dominate its contemporary life and will determine its fate.

One building is the Bank of China on the corner of Statue Square, a buff-coloured structure begun by the tottering Nationalist regime of Chiang Kai-shek and transferred by due process of Hong Kong law to the new Communist government of China in 1949, two years before it was completed. The building next door, completed in 1933, houses the main office of the century-old Hong Kong and Shanghai Banking Corporation, the chief financial power in the Colony, known to everyone here simply as The Bank. Both buildings are capped by ziggurat-like superstructures (the Bank of China by obvious intent is some 50 feet higher); and both display rows of tiny animal heads beneath the ziggurats—Chinese dragons complacently looking down from the Bank of China on to Hong Kong's main thoroughfare, British lions glowering from The Bank.

The juxtaposition of lion and dragon on two buildings so close together is obviously more than coincidental. Both beasts appear on Hong Kong's coat of arms: the shield itself is supported by a lion and dragon, while above it a second lion clutches a pearl. The symbolism is by no means strained. In 1841 Hong Kong—the Pearl of the Orient—was truly snatched by the British from the jaws of a negligent (and negligible) dragon. Today the Chinese can console themselves with the certain knowledge that the lion retains the pearl only by the dragon's goodwill—and the dragon knows it. Hong Kong survives as a British colony primarily because Peking, having recognized Hong Kong's multiple usefulness, is not eager to alter its status.

No rational Chinese government wants, just yet, to assume the burden of governing another troublesome Shanghai, a bourgeois city crammed with people jealous of their relative economic freedom and instinctively hostile to the Communists. More importantly, the Colony provides the People's Republic with more than a billion dollars a year in foreign exchange, through exports, remittances to families in China and

Oblivious to one of the fierce lions that symbolize British interests, a Chinese passes the entrance to the Hong Kong and Shanghai Banking Corporation, the Colony's largest commercial bank. The fruits of the man's small shopping transactions are slung from a bamboo pole in traditional fashion.

"invisible" earnings from its network of banks, shipping companies, insurance firms and other financial institutions, Hong Kong based, but owned outright or controlled by Peking.

A British lieutenant-colonel, commanding an armoured unit in Hong Kong, once told me: "I couldn't move a single tank against a Chinese attack if the local people co-operated with them. All it would take is a half-dozen buses and lorries blocking key road junctions in the New Territories—and my force would be totally immobilized." That was in the 1950s. Then there was at least the powerful presence of the American Seventh Fleet to make a would-be aggressor think twice before launching an invasion. Since then the Colony has become completely indefensible against assault by modern arms. China could force the British out of Hong Kong without firing a shot.

"This is the only beleaguered outpost in the world that could be taken by three or four telephone calls," a senior British civil servant said to me. Yet, curiously, the prospect of such an easy conquest has come to be much more remote than it was in the 1950s, when armed resistance, however ineffectual ultimately, was expected. The Chinese apparently desire no change in the status quo, and they have enjoined from disruptive activities the labour unions, commercial institutions, newspapers and strong-arm squads that are at their command in Hong Kong.

The fundamental policy of the Hong Kong government has been to placate the Chinese whenever it can and as far as it can without surrendering its independence. By the government's deliberate decision, the Colony (or Territory as they prefer to describe it at the official level) has been Sinicized: wherever possible, local Chinese have been appointed to senior posts in government departments and even in the once purely white Government Secretariat, the heart of Hong Kong's administration. These concessions, plus the fact that Hong Kong depends heavily on China for water and food supplies, mean that Peking can do much as it pleases—as long as it does not render the Colony unprofitable, an eventuality the Communists themselves would abhor. Certainly the possibility of the balance of power being reversed so dramatically in China's favour was inconceivable in the late 19th Century when Britain's star was still in the ascendancy and the Chinese Empire was undergoing its undignified and gory death throes.

The two worlds of which Hong Kong is composed began to clash in the 17th Century when importunate European merchants beseeched the Imperial Court in Peking to be allowed to trade freely with China. They were sent packing. A century later a British emissary, Lord Macartney, approached the Dragon Throne bearing all manner of gifts, among which were listed a planetarium, a hot-air balloon, scientific instruments, and assorted clocks and watches. He too sought establishment of "normal

Sited cheek-by-jowl across the street from the domed Supreme Court in Victoria, the Hong Kong and Shanghai Banking Corporation and the slightly taller Bank of China represent the local financial strongholds of Britain and the People's Republic respectively. The Bank of China mainly deals in foreign exchange.

trade and diplomatic relations". The 82-year-old Emperor Ch'ien Lung dismissed him with a sweeping Edict addressed to King George III: "As to what you have requested in your message, O King, namely to be allowed to send one of your subjects to reside in the Celestial Empire to look after your country's trade, this . . . definitely cannot be done. We have never valued ingenious articles, nor do we have the slightest need of your country's manufactures. You, O King, should simply act in conformity with our wishes by strengthening your loyalty and swearing perpetual obedience [to the Emperor] so as to ensure that your country may share the blessings of peace."

The lesson of China's unbreachable self-satisfaction and aloof disdain for money-grubbing foreigners was driven home again in 1816 by the treatment accorded another British mission. This time the Chinese Emperor (Ch'ien Lung's successor) would not grant the British ambassador an audience unless the Englishman agreed to kowtow—literally touch his forehead to the floor as a sign of submission. The ambassador refused, and went home without seeing the Emperor. Still, the stubborn British continued to be lured by the golden mirage of a vast China market.

If the British were avid, the Chinese were not quite so indifferent to the profits of commerce as they pretended to be. In 1557 they had ceded minuscule Macao to the Portuguese as a trading base, and a century later they had allowed a European trading settlement to be established at Canton in an area of about one-sixth of a square mile on the banks of the Pearl River. But the latter concession was most grudgingly made. The European foreign devils were permitted to stay in their Canton "factories", buildings that contained living accommodation as well as offices and warehouses, only from October to May. They were subject to strict curfew at night and not allowed to move about in large groups by day. They were forbidden to possess weapons or to get drunk, and they were denied the right to bring in their wives, whose presence might have given the settlement an air of permanence.

The fact is that the avowedly non-commercial Chinese—who divided human society into four descending classes, with the scholar-official at the top and the merchant at the bottom—were proud and extremely canny traders. By the 1830s, China was exporting to Europe and the United States large quantities of tea, dried rhubarb, silks, furs, lacquerware and porcelain, while importing only a trickle of novelties such as clocks and music-boxes. The consequent drain on sterling seriously unbalanced the finances of the Victorian British, who combined a passion for tea with a healthy respect for the laxative quality of rhubarb.

Only one commodity offered a ready solution to the imbalance of Britain's trade in the East: opium. China had an estimated two million opium users. The fact that the importation of opium was banned made illicit trade in it all the more profitable. The sale of opium to the Chinese

Victoria Peak forms a majestic backdrop for American, French and British ships in the growing port of Hong Kong, as painted by an unknown artist around 1850.

came in July, 1839, when a party of British sailors, on shore leave in Kowloon, were involved in a drunken brawl with local fishermen. A Chinese was killed in the affray, and Commissioner Lin demanded that the killer be handed over at once to stand trial in a Chinese court. When Captain Elliot refused to comply (in fact, the culprit was never identified), Lin retaliated by driving the British residents out of Macao. They retreated across the Pearl River estuary to Hong Kong. Soon thereafter, Royal Navy cutters and Chinese junks were exchanging cannon fire off Kowloon. The Opium War had begun—more a punitive action than a war, since the British merely launched a naval expedition to present a show of strength, by blockading the Canton River and occupying the Chusan Islands off the mouth of the Yangtze.

In January, 1841, some 14 months after the war started, peace terms were negotiated by Elliot and Commissioner Lin's successor, the Manchu mandarin Kishen, who agreed that China should pay an indemnity of $4.5 million and cede Hong Kong as a new centre of British trade. Six days later a naval landing party hoisted the flag at Possession Point. But the proclamation of a new British colony was premature. The Emperor repudiated the unsigned agreement, and so another expedition had to be launched to bring the Chinese dragon to heel. This time the punishment was more severe—and so were the penalties for peace. In 1842, by the terms of the Treaty of Nanking, China agreed to pay $16 million to the British as compensation and cede to them the island of Hong Kong in perpetuity. On June 26 of the following year, the island was formally declared a British Colony, with Sir Henry Pottinger, soldier and explorer, as its first Governor.

Hong Kong's growth began from the moment Elliot negotiated his aborted agreement with Commissioner Kishen. European merchants were immediately attracted to the island by his declaration that protection would be extended to subjects and ships of all foreign powers, and in June, 1841, they were further encouraged by his announcement that Hong Kong would be a free port without any duties levied on trade. At the same time, thousands of Chinese arrived from the mainland to seek work. In four years the island's population jumped from under 6,000 to nearly 24,000; Chinese outnumbered the Europeans, including the British military forces, by 20 to one.

During those years of gradual expansion British politicians continued to argue that the acquisition of Hong Kong was a major blunder and that the Chusan Islands would have made a better base for the China trade. Hong Kong was notorious for its typhoons and tropical diseases (storms in 1841 flattened the first British housing development, and fever killed hundreds of Europeans, mostly British soldiers, in the early years). Law enforcement was a constant problem because British and Chinese concepts of law were so completely different. In 1844 the recently arrived

Colonial Treasurer Robert Montgomery Martin ruefully reported that he could not see this "small barren unhealthy and valueless island" ever running at a profit. But the opium-smuggling merchants never had reasonable cause for complaint. Their business was booming: in 1844, the new Governor, Sir John Davis, deplored the fact that "almost every person possessed of capital who is not connected with government employment is employed in the opium trade".

Opium—or "foreign mud" as some Chinese called it—made Hong Kong and sustained its growth. English officials often complained that the Colony was attracting "the scum of Canton", and the first Registrar-General, Samuel Fearon, commented with Victorian self-righteousness that thousands of the Chinese settlers in Hong Kong were "careless of moral obligations, unscrupulous, unrespected". But many Europeans were even less scrupulous in their dealings with the Chinese. As the Chinese population increased, frictions between the wholly disparate civilizations intensified and the danger of another clash between the lion and the dragon became acute.

In January, 1857, the British discovered an organized attempt to exterminate the entire European community by poisoning them one morning at their breakfast tables. The trouble had started in October of the previous year when the Cantonese authorities seized a lorcha—a hybrid ship with a Western-style hull and Chinese bat-wing sails—called *Arrow*. *Arrow's* legal status was as mixed as its design. She was Chinese-owned, Hong Kong-registered, and commanded by a British master. When his ship was confiscated and the crew imprisoned on trumped-up charges of piracy, the Hong Kong government extended its protection—and when the Chinese refused to release the crew and to apologize, Governor Sir John Bowring hastily ordered gunboats to bombard Canton.

Soon afterwards the Indian Mutiny diverted British forces to India; not until 1858 were the British again in a position to attack Canton. Meantime, the Chinese mistook inaction for weakness. Viceroy Yeh of Canton ordered the Chinese to sever all links and refuse all co-operation with the British. He went so far as to offer bounties for the heads of the more prominent Western "barbarians". In Canton, British buildings were burned and British wharves destroyed. Shipping food supplies to Hong Kong was prohibited (most pragmatic Chinese traders, however, ignored the boycott), and in Victoria itself placards exhorted loyal Chinese to unite in action against the foreign devils. Out of the hatreds thus stirred up came the poison attempt.

On the morning of January 15, some 400 Europeans in Hong Kong were sitting down to breakfast. For many of the English the menu included kippers, sausages or kidneys, fried eggs and bacon, and—significantly—tea and toast. (Ignoring the tropical climate, the Victorians stuck stubbornly to this culinary ritual and firmly resisted all "foreign muck".) That morning

The mutual contempt that infected Chinese and British alike during the Opium War (1839-42) is vented in these contemporary drawings. The Chinese saw the British as hairy "foreign devils" who breathed noisome tobacco fumes (above), while a British cartoonist derided the fighting ability of the foe by depicting an armed Chinese sailor floating out to do battle seated on an inflated pig's skin.

there was a foul taste to the bread, all of which came from the same bakery in the Wanchai district. Subsequent chemical analysis proved that every loaf, white and brown, had been loaded with arsenic.

Characteristically, the Chinese had overdone it. The quantity of arsenic in the yeast was so great that it was immediately vomited up by many of those who swallowed it. No deaths were positively attributed to arsenic-poisoning, although some Europeans suffered unpleasant side-effects, either real or imagined. For many weeks thereafter the community trembled in a state of near-panic and self-imposed starvation.

The Europeans railed at the mandarins of Canton who apparently had contrived the outrage, and their anger against the Hong Kong police for lack of vigilance ran almost as high. There were demands that all suspects be hanged without trial. Governor Bowring, a tolerant and enlightened civil servant, rejected the demands and the bakery owner was acquitted for lack of evidence. But 52 of the bakery workers were confined in a police station lock-up only 15 feet square, and although 10 were finally brought to trial, the remaining 42 stayed cooped up there for nearly three weeks until their deteriorating physical condition forced their release. Arrests and deportations finally totalled around 750. During the year of the Great Poisoned Loaves Plot more than 26,000 Chinese left the Colony, nearly double the number who had emigrated the year before. Most of them went to California or Australia.

Before the poison plot, Sir John Bowring had been planning to prepare Chinese for appointment to government positions. Now the anger of the solid British mercantile class, which denounced him for "pandering to the Chinese", compelled him to abandon the scheme. He continued his attempts to establish schools for Chinese and Eurasians, and he kept trying to eliminate the rampant corruption in government, where European civil servants rapaciously squeezed Chinese petitioners. But his good-hearted reform campaign was doomed, as much by Chinese attitudes as by British antagonism. The Chinese, as he observed, expected to pay cumshaw—bribes—for access to the bureaucrats and were unwilling to testify in court against those in authority for fear of later reprisals. As Bowring put it, after finally securing London's approval to teach European civil servants Chinese: "We rule in ignorance, they obey in blindness."

Things were not quite that bad. Nonetheless, Bowring's assessment reflected the constant misunderstandings that plagued Britain's rule of Hong Kong. Moreover, the period of his administration exemplified the constant swing between benevolence and suppression in Britain's treatment of the Chinese. Equally characteristic was the alternating compliance and defiance of the Orientals. For if the British did not understand the Chinese, no more did the Chinese understand the British.

Normally political or commercial issues were what inflamed Chinese-European relations. But in 1894 it was an act of God that set the foreigners and the Cantonese against each other. Bubonic plague—the Black Death of medieval Europe—swept over the Colony. Within a few months, more than 2,000 persons died out of a total population of 240,000. No cure was known at the time, but simple British efforts to quarantine victims and the disease were thwarted because the Chinese concealed both illnesses and deaths.

When hundreds of British redcoats began a house-to-house search for victims, the Chinese concluded that the soldiers were actually body-snatchers in the service of Western doctors who wanted guinea-pigs for experiments. Propaganda originating in Canton inflamed that fear and encouraged even greater fears. Western doctors, the Hong Kong Chinese were convinced, habitually stole vital organs—especially the eyes of new-born babes—to make magical potions. Once again, posters inscribed in elegantly literary Chinese exhorted the populace to resist British sanitary measures in the name of patriotism. Riots and a Chinese exodus to Canton (itself badly infected) reduced the Colony to a moribund state; civic and commercial life almost ceased.

The worst of the plague was over by the end of 1895. But five years later anti-European posters were again being plastered all over Hong Kong. This time the Chinese propagandists were attacking the "British imperialists" for having joined forces with Japan and six Western nations in marching on Peking to relieve the Legation Quarter, then under siege by a fanatical sect known as Boxers which had as its motto "Protect the Country, Exterminate the Foreigners". The ensuing riots in Hong Kong were relatively small in scope, but the alternating pattern of periodic clashes and reconciliations had now been set.

In 1911 the overthrow of the imperial regime plunged China into chaos, but Hong Kong was relatively undisturbed. The Colony served as a neutral, peaceful haven for refugees from all the factions grappling for control of the mainland. As China reunified under a republican government, however, resentment towards the foreign presence increased again, and in 1925 a general strike virtually paralysed the Colony for an entire year. It was provoked when British soldiers fired on nationalistic Chinese demonstrators as they stormed the British- and French-held island of Shameen, the site near Canton of the original European factories. A new ingredient had been introduced into the cauldron: self-consciously militant chauvinism incited and directed by the Chinese Nationalist and Communist parties, then briefly in alliance.

The Japanese invasion of Manchuria in 1931 pushed the pendulum back. Needing friends, the Chinese government became increasingly amenable towards the British. In 1941, when the Japanese invaded Hong Kong, the lion and the dragon drew even closer together in resistance to the common enemy. Chinese, Eurasians and Europeans fought side by side for nearly three weeks within the Colony's ill-armed, undermanned forces,

Barren Island to Industrial Giant

1841	Union Jack hoisted on Possession Point after Hong Kong Island is claimed by Britain during a break in Sino-British Opium War (1839-1842)
1842	Treaty of Nanking ends Opium War and cedes China's island of Hong Kong in perpetuity to British
1847	Parliamentary committee enquiring into Chinese trade expresses doubt that Hong Kong can ever become a commercial centre
1850s	Hong Kong receives first flood of immigrants fleeing upheaval of China's Tai Ping Rebellion, ignited by famine and corruption of Manchu dynasty
1856	British-skippered Arrow is seized by Cantonese authorities for alleged piracy, re-opening Anglo-Chinese conflict
1857	Chinese bakery tries to poison European residents in Hong Kong
1860	Convention of Peking ends hostilities and cedes Kowloon and Stonecutters Island to Hong Kong
1888	Victoria Peak tram begins operation
1894	Plague sweeps over Colony, taking more than 2,000 lives
1898	The New Territories, leased to Hong Kong for 99 years under another Convention of Peking
1900	Rioting occurs in Hong Kong as zealots of Boxer Rebellion try to rid China of foreigners
1904	Reclamation of land greatly enlarges Victoria's Central District
1911	Revolution in China overthrows Manchu dynasty and results in fresh influx of refugees to Hong Kong
1912	Hong Kong's railway link with China, the Kowloon-Canton Railway, completed
1925	General strike, protesting against British actions in China, disrupts Hong Kong life for a year
1930s	Sino-Japanese War encourages friendly Chinese relations with British; several hundred thousand new refugees cross into Colony
1941	Hong Kong surrenders to Japanese on Christmas Day and begins almost four years under occupation
1946	British civil government reinstated; Hong Kong begins recovery
1949	Proclamation of People's Republic of China on October 1 marks Communist victory in civil war and accelerates unparalleled flow of refugees into Hong Kong. Especially important are industrialists of Shanghai, who bring expertise and capital
1950-1951	U.S. and U.N. trade embargoes during Korean conflict severely inhibit Hong Kong's role as trading link between China and rest of the world. Colony begins its transformation from an entrepôt to a largely manufacturing economy
1953	Christmas Day conflagration leaves more than 50,000 Kowloon squatters homeless and spurs government to begin housing programmes
1960	Hong Kong economy in midst of boom, primarily fuelled by cheap but highly skilled labour
1962	Communist guards temporarily relax frontier control. Between May 1 and May 23 more than 60,000 Chinese refugees pour into Hong Kong
1967	Reacting to China's Cultural Revolution, Hong Kong Communists exploit labour disputes to stage anti-British riots
1971	Free primary education extended to all government Chinese-language schools
1973	Stock market crashes in March after phenomenal rise
1974	Chinese made co-equal with English in discussions of Colony's Legislative and Urban Councils. Hong Kong decides that, in future, all illegal entrants caught slipping in from China will be forcibly "repatriated"

On Hong Kong's coat of arms, officially adopted in 1959, one British lion and a Chinese dragon flank the trading ships that have traditionally helped to make the Colony one of the most prosperous ports in the world. Over them another lion holds the "Pearl of the Orient" signifying Britain's continuing dominion over the metropolis. This crest embellishes the façade of Hong Kong's City Hall.

but their gallantry availed little against the battle-tempered, well-armed Japanese war machine. Their joint resistance and subsequent shared suffering during the occupation united Hong Kong's expatriate and local inhabitants. Thereafter, Caucasians and Orientals were not to tangle with each other again in Hong Kong until the border clashes that accompanied the Communist-inspired riots in 1967.

I remember that year well. It was a trial of the spirit and the body. That summer, the Colony sweltered in 93°F heat intensified by 90 per cent humidity. The political atmosphere was even more heavily charged because the People's Republic of China was then tearing itself apart through that extraordinary movement, the Great Proletarian Cultural Revolution. In China, millions of angry adolescents called Red Guards clashed with one another and with the People's Liberation Army. Their slogan was: "Destroy all old habits, customs, manners and culture!" In Hong Kong, where Maoist zealots seized upon a legitimate local labour dispute to demonstrate their own loyalty to the Cultural Revolution, the battle-cry was: "Topple British imperialism! Destroy the white-skinned pigs and their yellow running-dogs."

Violence erupted when the Maoist militants, gratuitously aligning themselves with the industrial strikers, clashed with the police. The constables had already made their choice. They were fighting for their homes and their families, and almost incidentally to preserve British rule. Like the police, the great majority of the Chinese population came to a repugnant conclusion: colonial rule was preferable to the mindless disorder that was convulsing China.

In Victoria, I watched the Maoist minority hurl itself against the wicker shields of the riot police. The Colony was in a state of internal siege, and all of us who remained took precautions that, in retrospect, may appear extravagant or even comical. One night my wife accompanied me in our car to the cable office where I was to file a story. I left her sitting in the car clutching a *kukri*, a Gurkha knife, and pondering my mildly hysterical instructions: "If someone puts his hand in the window, cut it off!" After a time we all became accustomed to the tension.

Throughout the long, fevered summer, casualties among the security forces were significantly higher than among the Maoists. In one memorable clash the police formed a cordon outside the Hilton Hotel to block mobs marching up Garden Road to Government House. Although continually reviled and manhandled, the constables stood firm for hours, following orders to restrain themselves, whatever their personal inclinations. When the command to charge was finally given, they dispersed the rioters who had been kneeing them in the groin and gouging at their eyes and noses. Equal self-control was displayed on the China frontier as Maoists began throwing stones at border police. But when Communist machine-guns

As a medal-bedecked band master sets the tempo (above), a British Light Infantry battalion marches in place on the parade ground-cum-basketball court (right) of the Gun Club Barracks in Kowloon. The battalion is part of Britain's commitment to the security of Hong Kong; along with three Gurkha battalions, it assists civil forces in patrolling the Chinese border.

were briefly fired it was time for a more positive show of strength. The government sent up reinforcements: tough Gurkhas armed with their wickedly curved *kukris*. There was no more shooting. Finally, after the Maoist campaign in Hong Kong had deteriorated into random planting of bombs and booby traps that killed only Chinese victims, and Canton itself had been partly "pacified" by the People's Liberation Army, the Colony's misguided militants were called off by the Communists.

Even now memories of that summer can raise hairs on the back of my neck. My wife and I had acquired courage over the years learning how to wage constant battle against the baby cobras that infested our garden; but I began to despair when a neighbour called to warn me to get my wife, my eight-year-old daughter and my five-year-old son out of the house "because there's a bomb in the middle of your road".

A few weeks earlier, a powerful businessman had asked me frantically: "What can we possibly do when half a million Red Guards march across the border?" He flatly refused to believe that the threat was by that time only imaginary. Demonstrating the fearful new respect Communist China had inspired in once smug Hong Kong, he joined the ignominious withdrawal of foreigners and wealthy Chinese who were suddenly called abroad on "urgent business" or to seek long-postponed medical attention. The panic was not only ill-informed but provoked support for the Maoists among the poor who felt themselves deserted.

After three months of internal battles the Colony was ready to return to business as usual. In the 1970s, this meant a stock market soaring to spectacular new heights and plummeting to no less spectacular lows, and

another campaign more determined than Bowring's to quash the corruption that had spread to almost every field of human endeavour. It meant, too, continuing British efforts to woo the Chinese community, which has a short memory. The lion and the dragon were again living in proximate peace, but as ever, they watched each other warily.

Ever since the 1840s Hong Kong has been at the centre of immense social and political storms, feeling their winds tangentially, and receiving their flotsam and jetsam. Yet the Colony has not been gravely shaken by the successive awesome upheavals between East and West. Relatively sheltered, except during the war years, the minuscule territory has been left to evolve its own unique society, in which the two civilizations meet on roughly equal terms. Formal British political ascendancy and the rapid development of Western techniques in fields ranging from shipbuilding to banking have been balanced by the weight of the Chinese in numbers (98 per cent of the Colony's four-and-a-half million population) and by the adaptability of these industrious people in learning to use everything from steam-engines to computers.

Hong Kong has become a social, political and economic laboratory where practical—though unintentional—experiments in social evolution are continuously conducted in an atmosphere of high pressure created by the Colony's compactness, large population and intense vitality. Neither wholly Eastern nor entirely Western, it is *sui generis*—a phenomenon never seen previously and never likely to be duplicated.

In the mid-1950s I listened to a middle-aged American tourist discovering that reality while making the 12-minute Star Ferry passage from

Kowloon to Hong Kong Island. "Can you tell me where Chinatown is?" he asked with earnest naiveté.

The attractive Chinese girl seated beside him smiled gently. "Don't move a single damned inch," she replied in the Indiana accent acquired from her American foster-mother. "You're in it—Chinatown East."

That is a highly accurate description of Hong Kong. It is even more aptly descriptive because it embodies a paradox—and the Colony is rich in paradoxes. More traditionally Chinese than any other city in Asia, it is also more Western than any other Asian city with the exception of Tokyo.

Over the years Hong Kong's two chief communities, European and Chinese, have certainly drawn closer together. Representatives on both sides daily cross the yawning cultural chasm, and neither community would today accept the Victorian assertion that "it is the destiny of one race to rule, and the fate of the other to be ruled". Essentially, however, the Europeans and Chinese live side by side rather than with each other. More than two million Chinese speak no foreign language, while the number of Chinese-speaking foreigners is still very small. In their fundamental customs and attitudes, the two communities remain worlds apart.

The British have tried to impose their own standards of morality on the Chinese, but the endeavour has proved neither wholly successful nor particularly harmonious. Most Chinese, for example, still go to court not to establish truth or to maintain justice, but simply to win. By their reasoning, perjury is a perfectly normal and even laudable action when it advances one's own interests or the interests of one's friends. Presumably even-handed British justice, often distorted in practice, is still struggling to establish itself as the norm among a people conditioned to regard magistrates and tax-collectors with equal suspicion.

The same resistance to British influence has persisted in the medical field. Practitioners of traditional Chinese medicine are still preferred to Western physicians by many Hong Kong people. Moreover, since Confucius considered the human body a sacred legacy from one's ancestors, a gift not to be altered in any way, only the new generation of Chinese will donate to blood banks. Yet almost all Chinese avow nearly supernatural faith in the efficacy of injections, regardless of the contents of the syringe.

In its language, folkways and culture, Hong Kong is a robust living fossil, or, to stretch a metaphor, a vigorous fly preserved not in amber but in ultra-modern plastic. Only in Hong Kong do polygamous Chinese marriages and concubinal relationships contracted before 1971 still enjoy full legal status (both the Chinese Nationalists and Communists had decreed monogamy many years earlier). In 1974 the Cantonese dialect, itself a living fossil that preserves some of the pronunciation of the Tang Dynasty (A.D. 618-907), was made an official language, co-equal with English in the discussions of the Colony's vest-pocket Legislative and Urban Councils. Everywhere else—in their Motherland and overseas—

At the peak of his success How Qua, a wealthy Chinese merchant, sat for this portrait around 1835. History holds that he was the wiliest member of the Co-hong, a small group of Canton middlemen to whom the emperor of China granted a monopoly on trade with foreigners, in exchange for a share of their profits. In spite of the hefty payoff to the throne, How Qua exploited the monopoly so deftly that he amassed a multi-million dollar fortune.

Chinese have been abandoning dialects for *kuo-yu* (national language) which is based upon the speech of Peking and which has for centuries been spoken—with local variations—by three-quarters of China's people.

In a society so stubbornly Chinese there is a need for go-betweens, and this all-important function has long been filled by the so-called "compradors", a term derived from the Portuguese word meaning "to purchase" or "to provide". For many years few Europeans were proficient in Cantonese or other Chinese dialects, and hardly any understood the labyrinthine intricacies of the Chinese community in Hong Kong. So the great trading firms depended on the services of compradors: Chinese or Eurasians who had fluent English and good business acumen.

For the most part compradors have been upright, efficient men discharging a difficult, but highly lucrative function. A celebrated few have become super-compradors, key figures in the Colony such as Sir Robert Ho Tung, who was the acknowledged leader of the Chinese community before his death in 1956 at the age of 94. A Eurasian born of a Chinese mother and a European sea-captain, Ho Tung became a multi-millionaire and in 1915 was knighted by the British Crown for his services to Hong Kong as a senior executive of Jardine, Matheson and Co., the Colony's premier *hong*, or trading firm. Like the Lees, the Los and the Moks— super-compradors whose names have commanded respect—Sir Robert was the link between the Chinese and the British, the essential connecting rod that made Hong Kong work.

Much of the comprador's old role is played today by the Chinese who function as government district officers. They keep an ever more sensitive administration informed of the people's sentiments and interpret the sometimes bewildering actions of the government to the populace. The understanding they promote helps in the unending battle to keep crime, for which Hong Kong has been notorious from its beginnings, within reasonable limits. I say reasonable limits because no informed belonger— Chinese or European, official or non-official—believes that organized crime and corruption can be completely eliminated from this highly complex society constantly subjected to new strains.

This brings us to the ultimate irony that emerges in assessing Hong Kong's origins and the impact of inevitable change on the metropolis. Today, the Colony's greatest law enforcement problems stem from drug abuse— chiefly heroin addiction. Heroin, of course, is made from opium. Thus, the Hong Kong government now spends tens of millions of dollars every year to suppress traffic in the drug (and its derivatives) that was the original reason for the Colony's existence, and, for more than half a century, its chief source of revenue.

Hong Kong is paying the price for having acted too weakly and too late. In 1913 the government established its own opium monopoly, producing and selling a weakened product. This subtle scheme to wean addicts on to less potent doses proved to be folly. It did not discourage opium smoking. It did encourage opium pushers to seek even greater profits by illegally supplying addicts who craved stronger supplies.

In 1946, the importation of opium and its derivatives was at last prohibited by law in Hong Kong. But as the authorities closed down more and more opium dens, so more and more addicts switched to the more dangerous heroin because it could be used without creating the distinctive aroma that makes opium-smoking so easy to detect. Turning opium into heroin is an elaborate business, requiring complex laboratory equipment and supplies of chemicals, but Hong Kong racketeers quickly rose to the challenge. In the 1950s they began to set up clandestine modern laboratories to produce heroin from opium smuggled in from Burma, Thailand and Laos, the so-called "Golden Triangle". And because heroin offered infinitely higher profits than opium, they had that much more scope for "buying" police and customs officials.

The results were disastrous. By the early 1970s, according to official figures, Hong Kong had 100,000 drug addicts—more than 2 per cent of the population. Among these, heroin addicts outnumbered opium addicts by almost 10 to one, whereas in the late 1960s only about half were addicted to the more lethal drug. Significantly, crime was also increasing, and more than half of all prisoners in the Colony's jails were addicted, forcing the authorities to set up treatment centres for convicted criminals.

While heroin addiction was taking hold in the Colony, Hong Kong's criminal entrepreneurs were also developing an international trade, exporting refined heroin to America and Europe. In their long war against these drug traffickers, police and customs officers (half the Colony's 1,100-strong customs service is committed full-time to anti-narcotics work) won several major battles. But each time the lawbreakers accommodated their techniques to changed circumstances. In the mid-1960s the authorities uncovered the main supply pipeline: massive quantities of opium and its derivative morphine were concealed within cargo arriving by sea from Thailand. So the smugglers began using Thai fishing trawlers for their deliveries. Even freshly caught fish were stuffed with narcotics. Drugs were passed to and from Hong Kong junks in international waters, or were left secured to marker buoys or dumped on one of the hundreds of uninhabited islands in the South China Sea for later collection.

By the mid-1970s, however, the Hong Kong authorities could fairly claim that they had been successful in .crippling, if not completely destroying, Hong Kong's international trade in heroin by stopping the import of the large supplies of opium needed to sustain it and by breaking up the more powerful syndicates that controlled it. Ng Sik-ho—known as "the Godfather" of the drug-redistribution rackets—was jailed for 30 years. The Colony might remain an administrative and financial base for international drug-trafficking networks, but it ceased to be a principal clearing-house for heroin distribution.

The internal drug problem, though, remains one of alarming proportions. Why cannot the authorities totally eliminate drug supplies in such a confined territory? Partly because it is impossible to check on every one of the many thousands of junks operating out of Hong Kong; more especially because a vast underground network of clannish Chinese residents block the authorities' efforts to track down and raid premises used for the manufacture, storage, sale or taking of drugs. Numerous Chinese guards and watchmen are stationed around drug retailing centres, especially in the Walled City of Kowloon—a tiny area of slum-dwellings that, because of a treaty dispute dating from 1898, is still under the control of China. There, the word is quickly relayed from stall to stall, door to door, as soon as a stranger appears.

In addition to maintaining an elaborate early warning system, the racketeers keep their drug supplies widely dispersed in small stores and operate a refinery in one place for only a short period before moving it on to a new location. The refineries, however, constitute the greatest risk of detection by the police, and consequently there has been an increasing tendency to import heroin already processed in Thailand.

Meanwhile, the government continues to finance major programmes for drug treatment and rehabilitation. But the breaking of widespread drug-addiction in the Colony is a sisyphean struggle—a new-style Opium War destined to be fought for as long as Hong Kong remains a capitalist society and has an enormous domestic market to attract the profiteers. Thus, history has turned full circle and poetic justice has been squarely served. The Colony created to export opium to China struggles desperately to prevent opium—and allied drugs—coming in from South-East Asia. And China, the original victim, has no drug problem at all.

At Home in the Water

At Sai Kung, a New Territories harbour where his family have anchored for generations, Tanka fisherman Ma Sui-sing and his mother study the weather.

The Ma family, whose waterborne way of life is explored on these pages, are members of an old and sturdily traditional ethnic group: the Tanka, or boat people. The Tanka form a majority of the Colony's floating population—the biggest concentration of boat-dwellers in the world—who live on junks anchored in Hong Kong's bays and inlets. Most still fish for a living. But to cling to their old ways they must endure hardship.

Eleven members of the Ma family share the four compartments of their 50-foot junk. Their 15-hour workday begins at 3 a.m. and may produce only enough fish for their own subsistence. As the lure of an easier life dilutes the younger generation's devotion to Tanka tradition, the floating population slowly dwindles. This trend has affected the Mas: their eldest son abandoned fishing for a factory job ashore.

Ma's wife, wearing oilskins and a high-crowned, wickerwork Tanka hat, sets out in a sampan.

Leaving the Ma junk, a neighbour poles a sampan along one of the lanes of open water that serve as "streets" for the traffic of the crowded floating village.

Watched by a visiting neighbour's tiny child, a young son of the Ma family bends almost double to climb through a narrow opening into the dark, cramped quarters of his floating home. Having lived all his life aboard a junk, he accomplishes the manoeuvre with graceful ease.

Two Ma boys tie short strings that will hold hooks on a new line. The pans keep the coils of nylon untangled.

Catching up on Vital Repairs

When at home, the Ma family spend most of their time—every afternoon, and all day if the weather is too bad for fishing—taking care of their equipment. They fish by the traditional Tanka method: the lines, each bearing a hundred hooks baited with small fish are attached to floats that are dropped into the sea each morning and picked up later. Lines frequently need to be mended or replaced, and tying on new hooks is a long and tedious process.

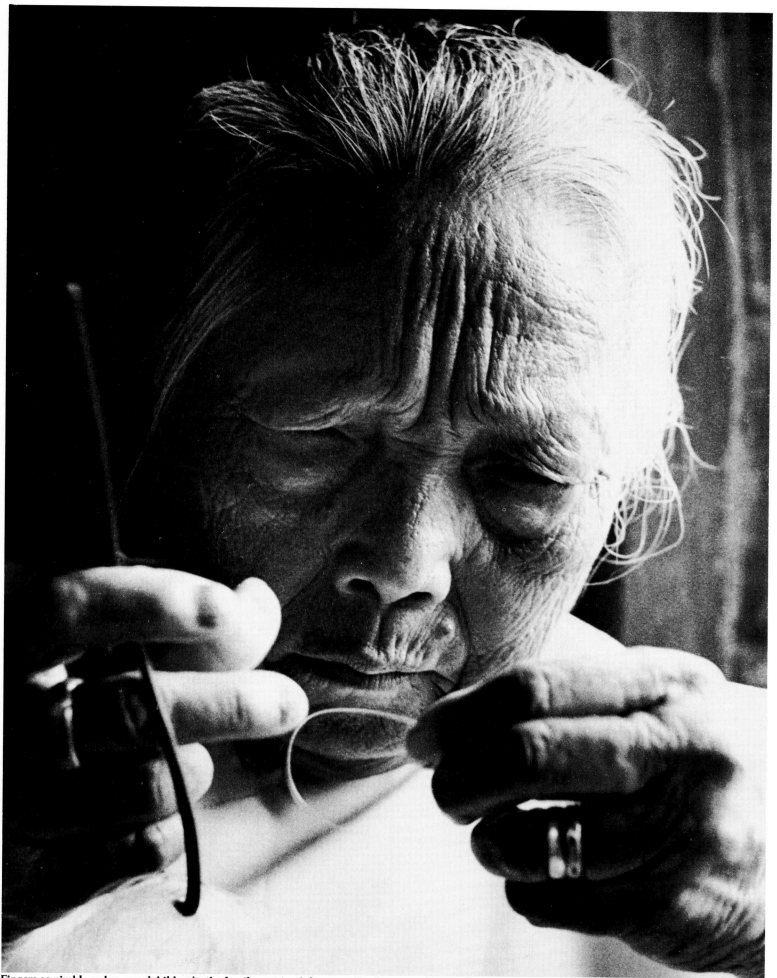

Fingers as nimble as her grandchildren's, the family matriarch fixes new hooks on to a line, a job she has done virtually every day for almost all her 85 years.

In the low-ceilinged main cabin of their junk, the Mas sit on the floor to share a meal, enjoying the warmth and conviviality characteristic of Tanka life.

3

Money-Mad Metropolis

When I first came to Hong Kong, the Colony superficially appeared to be approaching economic and political collapse. The atmosphere of crisis—of striving against fate, as it were—made the then mysterious territory all the more exciting to me. I was a very young reporter, the year was 1951 and there were good stories everywhere—the full-scale conflict in Korea, a smaller war rapidly expanding in Indo-China, and the uncertainty about the future of Taiwan, where the Nationalists lived in bitter exile. My sense of being at the centre of potentially world-shattering events charged the muggy Hong Kong air with excitement.

Never was a metropolis more alive with absurd anomalies. Here two nations that were at war in Korea maintained an armed truce and, more remarkably, continued mutually profitable commercial relations across a common border. British troops, including some from the Colony's garrison, had been posted to the United Nations' Command in Korea to fight the "Chinese People's Volunteers". But at the frontier between the New Territories and China's Kwangtung province, Communist border guards faced detachments of the Hong Kong police and neither side fired a shot in anger. Instead, they communicated with strained courtesy to facilitate the movement of people and goods between China and Hong Kong.

U.S. Navy warships, coming off patrol duty in the Yellow Sea or Taiwan Straits, tied up at the sombre black buoys in Victoria Harbour where Communist coasters and junks abounded. Their crews scattered for "Rest and Recreation" to the dives of Wanchai and Kowloon, and disported themselves with cheap liquor and willing bar girls. Each visit by a major American naval unit and her escorts left Hong Kong richer by several million dollars. And a substantial portion of that money—exactly how much no one knew—found its way through the Communist-owned Bank of China to the People's Republic, the enemy those men of the American navy were fighting.

In spite of the atmosphere of business as usual, Hong Kong lived in fear of imminent Chinese take-over. Many foreigners, private citizens as well as diplomats, had already taken the precaution of sending their wives and families away because they expected an attack from across the border. The New Territories had proved indefensible once before, when the Japanese struck in 1941, and everyone knew they would be again if the cocky new government in Peking threw even one or two of its many divisions against the few battalions that composed the Colony's garrison. Immediate subjugation might be forestalled by Anglo-American bombing

Neon advertisements for consumer goods, such as watches or radios, light up the evening in the Wanchai district. The Hong Kong government, placing a rare restraint on merchandizing vigour, bans flashing neon displays on the grounds that they pose a navigational hazard to planes landing at Kai Tak Airport.

of China's vulnerable cities, but that counter-strategy could ignite a Third World War, since the Chinese were at that time able to count on the support of the Soviet Union, then still their ally.

There seemed little reason to think that the situation would improve. Hong Kong's economy had been dealt a severe blow by the United States: by imposing an embargo on Chinese trade in December, 1950, the American government had prevented Hong Kong from exporting a wide range of goods from the People's Republic to the United States. Then, in May, 1951, the United Nations imposed an embargo of its own on the sale of strategic commodities to China, and this had an even more devastating effect. It drastically undermined Hong Kong's traditional standing as an entrepôt, or trading port (until the outbreak of the Second World War, Hong Kong had been among the greatest market-places of international trade in the world). Furthermore, the United Nations embargo created a period of stagnation during which Hong Kong had to adjust to its unnerving position in a limited war.

It would have boggled the mind then to predict that Hong Kong would not only survive, but escalate from being a trader of other people's goods to the status of one of the leading export "nations" of the world, where millionaires are more visibly numerous than anywhere else I have ever been. But before I begin to trace that astounding rise, I must fill in a few more of the details that led to Hong Kong's recovery and spelt the phenomenon of its economic success.

So many times in the 19th Century Hong Kong had experienced the same curious condition of not-war not-peace with China. Now, once again it sought to ride out an international storm. The government, perforce, strictly observed the U.N. embargo—at a cost of half its export market. At the same time the ban greatly increased the profits from smuggling and, in consequence, it seemed that half the rascals and entrepreneurs of Asia were lured to the Colony.

To complicate matters further and undermine the economy still more, illegal refugees from China were pouring into the Colony at the rate of tens of thousands a year. This influx of people, unparalleled in Hong Kong's history, had first escalated dramatically in 1948 as the Communists gained the ascendancy in the civil war against the forces of the Nationalist government. Very soon the steady stream had risen to a veritable tidal wave and, during 1949 and the following spring, almost three-quarters of a million refugees arrived. By the end of 1950 the population (a mere 600,000 in 1945) had been swelled to 2,360,000. The never-ebbing tide had to be checked, or the economy would have been wrecked completely. But marine police had an impossible task in patrolling 400 miles of coastline, and the frontier guards could never watch day and night every section of the border's 17 twisting miles.

Mass-produced statuettes of the Buddhist Goddess of Mercy and God of War join an effigy of Jesus Christ in a display at a Hong Kong souvenir shop. Such stores sell hundreds of different effigies to tourists and to Hong Kong residents who want them for home shrines.

I remember my first tour of the border under the guidance of an amiable British police inspector. We drove to one of the forts on a hill overlooking border posts flying the red flag of the People's Republic, then descended towards the Shum Chun (Deep River), which forms most of the boundary between Hong Kong and China. At four in the afternoon, the young inspector's binoculars picked up movement on the Hong Kong bank. Our Land Rover jounced over the rutted trail and came to a halt beside a bedraggled, emaciated figure. He was a 34-year-old farmer, dripping wet and exhausted after swimming the 150-foot-wide river to the sanctuary he thought Hong Kong would provide.

"This one," said the inspector regretfully, "will have to go back. If we catch them crossing, we've no choice. Pity we weren't a few minutes later."

The farmer, I learned, had found himself denounced and persecuted by Communist officials as a "landlord-exploiter" because he held title to an acre-and-a-half paddy-field and seven pigs. In an effort to follow up the story I tried to ascertain the disposition of his case. But my repeated inquiries yielded no specific information, only the bland reply from the Government Information Services that it was difficult to check on the case of an individual refugee. "Actually," a British information officer confided to me, "our records are in a fearful mess!" I have since then suspected—almost to the point of certainty—that hospitable Hong Kong managed to evade its own regulations and allow the man to stay. At considerable risk to its own interests, Hong Kong was still fulfilling its century-old function of providing refuge to the human debris cast up by China's political and economic upheavals.

As the human flood of illegal refugees continued throughout the 1950s, Hong Kong appeared ever more certainly doomed to cataclysmic upheavals—as if it were a ship so overloaded that it must inevitably founder in the South China Sea. The housing shortage was most frightening of all. Thousands squatted on rooftops, on tenement stairways, on sidewalks; hundreds of thousands encamped along the ridge-lines of hillsides in ramshackle shanties of bamboo, corrugated iron, wooden boxes—any materials they could scavenge. The sanitary problems were appalling enough, but in addition to disease the squatters were at the mercy of typhoons and fire. When the rains came, their hovels plunged down the slopes amid avalanches of mud. When it was dry, fires swept through the tinderboxy settlements and left thousands homeless.

The worst single disaster was to come on Christmas Day, 1953, when more than 50,000 squatters lost their homes in a conflagration that roared through the tiers of shanties in the Upper Kowloon district of Shek Kip Mei. That great fire at last spurred the government into launching a resettlement programme: clearing the worst of the shanty towns, providing vast public housing estates for the homeless at rents they could afford, and generally trying to integrate the refugees into the community. Drastic concessions

Toys Unlimited

Among the many evidences of Hong Kong's manufacturing and mercantile wizardry is the Colony's place among the world leaders in the output of toys. Its 3,000 toy factories, large and small, turn out roughly a million different types of playthings every year. A few examples of that astonishing range are here presented as a mosaic composed of products in various stages of completion. In the top row (far right), chicly coiffured doll heads are packed in sachets to protect their nylon permanent waves; other heads, like the harvest of a guillotine, wait to be fitted with wigs or to have their over-long eyelashes clipped to proper length (centre row, first left). The parts of some of the mechanical toys have not yet acquired a discernible identity. The wheels choking a bin on the top row (centre) are destined for miniature locomotives, while the array of bright red mouldings in the centre row (second left) are the sides of motor cars.

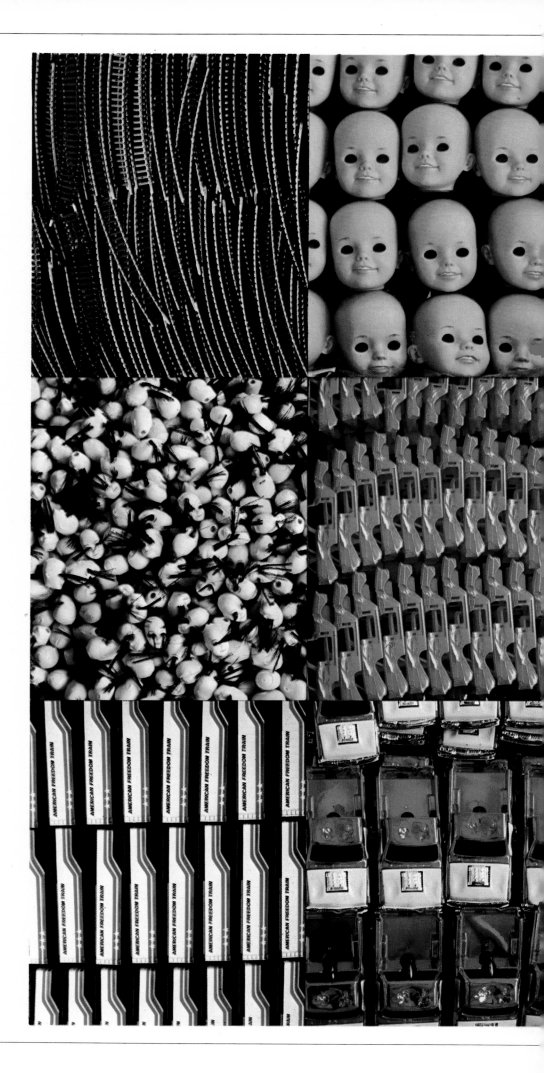

were made in the interests of building quickly and cheaply. The new, barrack-like homes, starkly utilitarian, were uniform blocks of reinforced concrete, six and seven storeys high, with communal washrooms shared by hundreds of people. Nevertheless, it was a significant breakthrough. For the first time the Colonial administration was accepting responsibility for housing the refugees. Once they had done so, it logically followed that they should take a degree of responsibility for the general well-being of the refugees in terms of medical care, education and conditions of labour. Within 20 years of starting the resettlement programme they provided homes for 1.8 million people in 56 public housing estates, and more than 41 per cent of the entire population of Hong Kong were living in government or government-subsidized accommodations.

However, such an energetic revival appeared most unlikely when I first came to Hong Kong. The Colony's trade was being strangled by the embargoes; economists were telling us of the likelihood that the territory would fast become a "disaster area", crowded with a million starving and homeless refugees. Still, a few incredibly inspired entrepreneurs, from China and from the West, accurately read "boom and prosperity" in their crystal balls. The rest of us were so profoundly concerned with the Korean War and the possibility of wider Chinese aggression that we could barely appreciate the enormous significance of the new circumstances and their bearing on Hong Kong's future.

Ironically, the uninvited million Chinese who so alarmed Hong Kong were to prove its salvation. They would make economic survival possible by providing the capital, industrial expertise and skilled, cheap labour force necessary for Hong Kong to develop for the first time a thriving export trade of its *own* manufactures. The miracle of Hong Kong's industrial revolution was about to begin.

"Economic miracle" is a term perhaps too casually bandied about by financial journalists, in much the same way that sportswriters refer every few years to the fight or the match of the century. But I offer no apology for using it in respect to Hong Kong's recovery. Nothing less will serve to sum up the progress of a minuscule territory which—without any local source of energy, with very few mineral resources and with limited space for factory development—has emerged as one of the great manufacturing centres of the world.

Consider just a few simple facts. In 1945 the Colony was economically— and physically—in ruins after four years of Japanese occupation. In less than five years it rebuilt to new high levels the entrepôt trade on which its survival had depended for more than a hundred years. When that economic base was shaken by the Korean War embargoes, the Colony was compelled to make its own exports and attempt to compete with countries vastly richer in natural resources and industrial experience. Hong Kong did more than compete. By 1959, some 70 per cent of its exports were domestic products (compared with 25 per cent in 1950). By the 1970s, the Colony was listed among the 20 leading "trading nations" of the world. It had become the world's largest exporter of garments, toys, plastic flowers and flashlights. It had a booming electronics industry, the world's second largest film industry (after India), and generally such a staggering range of products for export that "Made in Hong Kong" became a label as familiar as "Made in Japan".

Many factors contributed to Hong Kong's dynamic industrial revolution: its unrivalled location and deep-water harbour facilities; the fact that it already had all the necessary import-export machinery and know-how; its stable government, highly efficient banking and insurance facilities, low income tax and, generally, economic policies that traditionally favoured free enterprise and free trade. But the vital most valuable asset of all was the massive labour force arising from the refugee invasion—not just the sheer numerical strength of that force, but the quality and character also.

The vast majority of refugees in Hong Kong were desperately eager to make a new life for themselves and their families outside a Communist state. They were prepared to take any job, however lowly paid, rather than return to mainland China where the new-born People's Republic had not yet eliminated mass unemployment and starvation. Most were poorly educated, but they were incredibly industrious and they could be trained in skilled trades. Moreover, the bulk of them came from near-by Kwangtung province, as did the majority of Hong Kong's residents, and they therefore fitted easily into the existing society.

It was of great significance, too, that they did not constitute a labour force that was truly organized for power. In 1955, for instance, the Colony had 227 workers' unions, but they acted independently of each other and not one of them alone had the strength to bring an industry to a standstill. This was partly due to deeply ingrained political divisions and personal rivalries among the unions. It was also due to the basic character of the average Chinese workman. Then—much more than now, when a new generation of workers has asserted itself—trade union practice was a form of behaviour fundamentally alien to him. By tradition he was drawn to narrower, tight-knit institutions: the family unit, clans, secret societies, religious sects. By nature he was thrifty (except in his predilection for gambling), proud, and keen to preserve his independence.

Of course, Hong Kong's economic miracle could not have been worked without capital investment. But that, too, was in the main initially provided by refugees from China—most notably by Shanghai industrialists who anticipated the downfall of the Nationalist regime and prepared for it by arranging for newly ordered equipment to be diverted to Hong Kong. When the Communist forces marched on Shanghai in 1949, some capitalists there already had their escape route planned—and they took key

During a momentary lull at their impromptu business premises along a sidewalk in the Western District of Hong Kong Island, two vendors discuss the day's trading in trinkets, second-hand goods and old currency.

skilled workers with them. At that time textiles were the main product for China's biggest manufacturing centre, accounting for 62 per cent of the value of Shanghai's industrial output. Significantly, Hong Kong's industrial revolution was to be firmly based on textiles, beginning with cotton and eventually extending to woollen knitted goods and later to man-made fibres and garments made from them.

The sophisticated Shanghailanders were markedly different from other refugees arriving in Hong Kong. Their manners had been polished to a high sheen by the frictions within cosmopolitan Shanghai, and their commercial acumen had been honed to a sharp edge by that city's intense competition. The men wore expensive Western-style suits, and the lacquered women dressed in sheath-tight, slit-skirted cheongsams. But these new members of Hong Kong's Chinese élite were as indispensable to the industrial revolution as the great army of workers in their baggy, wrap-around Chinese trousers and black coolie tunics. In addition to their capital (which, in turn, encouraged foreign investment) they brought entrepreneurial skills of an exceptionally high calibre. They were quick to spot possible new markets, imaginative in trying experiments with new products, bold in pursuing their hunches.

Initially, Hong Kong's industrial revolution was fuelled by the ever-increasing demand for new housing. This spurred the growth of allied industries: the manufacture of cement, metal products, paints, plumbing fixtures, and furniture. Plastics and electronics came later. But the rapidly growing textile industry above all others, sustained the revolution. In 1954 it employed 30 per cent of Hong Kong's total work-force. Five years later textiles and clothing employed 44 per cent of the work-force and accounted for 52 per cent of Hong Kong's total domestic export earnings ($396 million). Entrepreneurs in the field earned personal fortunes running into many millions. The extent of their industrial affluence was forcefully driven home to me in 1970 when I heard a Shanghai-born textile magnate talking to an American who wanted to order 12,000 blouses. "Not enough to bother with," he said. "I sweep up more than that from the factory floor every week."

In the mid-1970s, even after being severely restrained by import quotas imposed by Western nations to protect their own textile manufacturers, the industry still accounted for 48 per cent of total export earnings ($4,600 million). And it was still employing more than half the industrial work-force.

The textile industry had special advantages. In a territory so desperately short of land, it could operate successfully in multi-storey premises, whereas heavy industry demanded larger sites. New factories were built and equipped with the most modern, most efficient machinery. Looms were kept in operation 24 hours a day, seven days a week, except over the Chinese New Year. In addition, many hundreds of cottage-industries provided cloth and goods of their own. It was an industry founded on

Workmen assemble a bamboo scaffold to take down a traditional Chinese New Year message emblazoned on the side of an office building in Central District. "A Prosperous New Year" is the literal meaning of the characters, but the greeting serves also as a declaration of the company's own recent good fortunes.

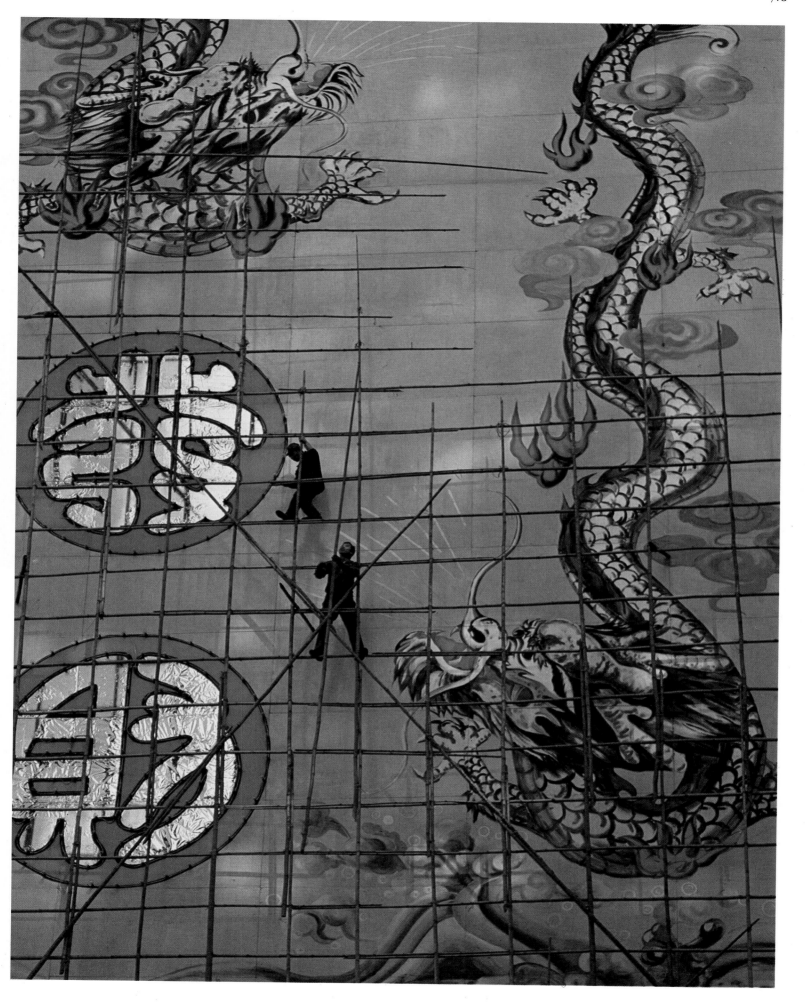

"sweated labour". For many years the labour force was largely over-worked and underpaid, without the benefit of many of the government regulations that today forbid, among other things, the employment in industry of children under 14 (younger children, however, may work at home). But this hard-earned expansion helped save Hong Kong. And it ensured that no one had to starve or remain unemployed.

Beyond sheer sweat and toil, three vital factors kept Hong Kong's industrial machinery in full operation: diversification, flexibility, inventiveness. Again and again, the manufacturing industries were threatened by increasing overseas competition, new trade barriers and changing demands. Some succumbed, but a great many survived because they responded so swiftly and shrewdly to new circumstances. When Hong Kong's cheap labour was undercut by that of Taiwan and South Korea, the Colony's industries escaped direct competition by turning to more sophisticated products.

From manufacturing simple transistorized radios, Hong Kong switched to higher quality sets and became, after Japan, the world's second largest exporter of radios. From cheap plastic toys and sand buckets, manufacturers progressed to radio-controlled toys, calculators with memory systems, computer components and electronic timepieces.

Complacency is the one luxury that Hong Kong industrialists have never been able to afford in this fiercely competitive open market-place. They must keep themselves constantly alert to the changing laws of supply and demand. Some years ago I met a Hong Kong businessman who had grown highly prosperous by manufacturing wigs (a major export until 1970). He abandoned the trade as soon as the demand for hairpieces fell sharply, and a few months later I heard he had set himself up successfully in a new business: canning shark's fin soup! An extreme example perhaps, but one that is nonetheless indicative of the quick-wittedness that kept the Colony's boom alive.

Thus it was that the business of Hong Kong became, more than ever, business. It might even be said, without too much hyperbole, that the religion of Hong Kong is now, also, business. The Colony is not merely un-ashamed of its dedication to the pursuit of money; it glories in mercantile devotion that transcends idolatory to verge upon spiritual exaltation. Hong Kong's Holy Grail is the Hong Kong dollar, a remarkably strong unit of currency which during most of the 1970s appreciated steadily not only against the weak pound sterling, but also against the U.S. dollar. The High Temple of this cult of money is the Hong Kong and Shanghai Banking Corporation. Its high priests are the directors of The Bank and of the great *hongs*, like Jardine, Matheson and Co., or Butterfield and Swire.

The lesser clergy—the money-changers who for decades carried the gospel to the people under the sacred dollar sign, cashing cheques and

Beribboned baskets of flowers from well-wishers decorate a jewellery shop in central Hong Kong on its opening day. Prosperity is likely, since the low cost of labour in the city—and the absence of tariffs on gems and precious metals—will enable the shop to price its creations at highly attractive levels.

issuing drafts dealing in foreign currencies—are rapidly shrinking in numbers, being superseded more and more by the system of computers, credit cards and telegraphic transfers. In their day of glory, however, they were an integral part of Hong Kong's commercial life, ubiquitous dealers who were fiercely competitive and intensely proud of dedicating their lives to the basic article of Hong Kong's continuing faith: that two tenths of a cent earned on every dollar which passed through their hands must inevitably lead to riches.

When my favourite money-changer was mulcted by his partners and forced out of the firm, he took his misfortune with resignation. "It was bound to happen," he said. His mortal sin had been inattention. And he recognized that the retribution—being cheated by his partners—was itself irrefutable evidence that he had personally failed in his moral responsibility, which was to shade all transactions in his own favour. His partners could not be blamed for taking advantage of his failure, it was almost their sacred duty. The price of fortune in Hong Kong's cut-throat world of commerce is indeed eternal vigilance.

The reward for such vigilance can be handsome: a good profit that the individual may largely keep. In the mid-Seventies the maximum rate of tax on earned income was only 15 per cent, and only 220,000 of Hong Kong's 4.5 million people paid any income tax at all. The low taxes, bountiful business opportunities, and deliberate lack of restraints on the acquisition, deployment and flow of money collectively made, of course, for a capitalist's paradise.

It is not difficult to spot the millionaires among the toiling masses. In Hong Kong, the surest measure of a man's wealth is the property he owns. I learned the truth of that maxim soon enough when I moved into a house on Shouson Hill Road, near Deep Water Bay, and met my neighbour and landlord, a Mr. Chow Yao. The man had started his working life as a gravedigger. Physically, he resembled an amiable, retired China Coast pirate. The most obtrusive ornaments in his sitting-room were a terracotta bust of his own dark skinned, rotund features and a two-foot-square enlargement of a coloured photograph of himself receiving the insignia of the M.B.E. (Member of the Most Excellent Order of the British Empire) from Queen Elizabeth II. Although obviously lacking both polish and a higher education, he was one of the most popular and respected millionaires in Hong Kong.

Mr. Chow was a multi-millionaire because, several decades ago, a wealthy Hong Kong family had rewarded him for faithful service by making him a gift of a small parcel of land in Shouson Hill Road. The land has soared in value to at least $1 million. It provided the financial base on which Chow Yao built elaborate and lucrative corporate structures. More appropriately, the ex-gravedigger invested some of his money in burial land, where a six-year tenancy of a six-by-three-foot grave plot can cost the surviving kin as much as $10,000, and long-term occupancy of a similar area will quite easily sell for anything up to $60,000.

Since the greater part of Hong Kong's 404 square miles is mountainous and unsuitable for development, the reason for ever-rocketing land prices is obvious. And, in the long-term, the government is the greatest beneficiary of all. By law the government owns all land in the Colony and it sells the leases (up to 75 years) at public auction to the highest bidder. Ever since the Colony was born, the sale of Crown Land leases has been a major source of government revenue. But today, with the prize sites long since sold, its annual revenue from land transactions, $26 million-plus, is only a fraction of the revenues from taxes on earnings and profits (well over $400 million) and not spectacularly more than the $24 million or so derived from the taxes on betting.

Meanwhile, property owners continue to seize opportunities to make astronomical profits. Early in the 1970s, for example, the cost of housing increased 200 per cent in a single year. Even millionaires thought twice about buying at that time. Raymond Chow, the dynamic Hong Kong movie mogul, hesitated to offer $400,000 for a house on a sixth of an acre next door to me. Two months later, when he made up his mind to buy, the price had reached $850,000.

The saddest millionaire I met was an American who wanted to buy a pleasant little house with a nice view. The seller hoped to exact an offer of only $300,000, but he was advised by his astute lawyer not to sell directly to the American but to go to auction because prices were escalating so fast. The American remained confident of acquiring the residence. Within five minutes the bids soared beyond the $1 million mark, and the American had long since dropped out. The property went to a Chinese banker. "I guess I'm not in his class," the American confessed ruefully. "But one thing really hurts. I understand he intends to use the house primarily for entertaining and for occasional weekend visits. Yet he's got a perfectly good penthouse on top of his bank!"

The wealth created by cheap labour—even if it was no longer as cheap as it used to be—has been conspicuously spent on some very spectacular fancies, such as the building of mock-Ming palaces, adorned with upswept tile roofs and monumental statuary like those in Peking's Imperial City, and with rooms varying from Japanese-style cubicles with sliding rice paper walls to Bavarian beer cellars, complete with mounted antlers on time-worn beams.

Hong Kong's prosperity is usually expressed in exuberant style. A man who made his fortune from Tiger Balm, an oily camphor-based concoction that many Chinese believe cures everything from headaches to leprosy, spent the money amassing one of the world's most precious jade collections, so large that he had to divide it between two mansions, one in Hong Kong, the other in Singapore. But my favourite excess involves a

A factory official draws an attentive audience as he adds a new notice to a caged array of job advertisements in the San Po Kong district of Kowloon. Many Hong Kong workers find industrial employment through such public notices, but recruitment for white-collar positions is mostly done through the Press.

millionaire who arranged to have one of his Rolls-Royce cars painted pink to match the dress his wife wore one evening to a party. His wife's white poodle was also dyed to match.

Some of the big spending, however, is more business investment than mere self-indulgence. The Chinese put an enormous value on "face" and pay to keep it up, just as Western businessmen recognize the monetary value of prestige and hire public relations firms to burnish their images. Sir Lawrence Kadoorie, multi-millionaire owner of the stately Peninsula Hotel knows that an apparently extravagant gesture can be profitable if it attracts wealthy clients to his expensive establishment. A few years ago I asked him whether it was true that he had 10 Rolls-Royces to pick up hotel guests at the airport. "No," he replied. "That's a gross exaggeration. We have seven Rolls-Royces and a spare."

When I first came to live in the Colony I was interested basically in two things: Chinese culture and the politics of Asia. As time wore on I began to realize that almost everyone I knew was either a businessman or someone waxing rich in the service of businessmen. Yet, with a caution and restraint that now bemuses me, I stood still for a whole decade while friends around me progressed steadily from Volkswagens or Austins to Cadillacs or Rolls-Royces, from holidays in Penang to villas in Portugal. But one can't live in Hong Kong forever without succumbing to the lure of "easy money". And so, belatedly, my wife and I agreed that our own pittance would be better invested in the booming Hong Kong economy than in a savings account.

Mass-produced Fantasy

In its ceaseless quest for riches, Hong Kong has hit upon a gold mine with its film industry. Large-scale profits began to flow in 1960 when Asia's largest film studio—Movietown—was built at Clearwater Bay in the New Territories and began churning out sensational pictures such as those touted here—one based on the martial art of Kung Fu, another offering sex and violence, and the third a historical epic about the Empress Dowager of China. By the 1970s, Movietown and other enterprises had made Hong Kong a world leader in film-making, with an output exceeding 200 motion pictures a year.

飛孟 軍冠戚 聲傅 龍狄 衛大姜

演主衛領

徹張

FIVE SHAOLIN MASTERS

少林五祖

品出司公影電弓長
CHIANGS FILM CO. PRESENT

Through a long-standing acquaintance, I had the benefit of free advice from multi-millionaire Eric Ho Tung, a grandson of Sir Robert, that super comprador of old. We didn't make a fortune under his guidance simply because he sternly and sensibly prohibited our essaying the high-flying ventures in which he himself took such a delight. Still, for the first time, and in spite of a shaky economic period of bank failures and political rioting in the Sixties, we did have the satisfaction of seeing our capital enjoy a steady if unspectacular growth. And then something phenomenal happened—the most extraordinary, all-round surge in share prices in the Colony's history.

It was January, 1972. The economic boom that had been in progress since the mid-Fifties had multiplied the Colony's total bank deposits nearly fivefold to a record level of $4,326 million (a 31 per cent rise over the previous year). Industrial expansion had started to forge ahead again. Suddenly and simultaneously, tens of thousands of ordinary folk— housewives, dockers, shopkeepers, waiters, professional men—had also accepted that it was foolish to leave money lying fallow in their deposit accounts. The word spread like a shanty-town fire that playing the stock market was one sure way to riches, and almost overnight Hong Kong was gripped by a stock-buying fever of epidemic proportions.

Directly or indirectly, the lives of almost everyone in Hong Kong were affected to some degree. Companies found it virtually impossible to recruit new staff to replace employees who had "retired" to concentrate full-time on buying and selling shares. A number of businesses closed down when their proprietors decided they could get a much higher return on their capital by speculating in stocks. Even private households were deprived as independent-minded maidservants left to devote their time to consultations with their stockbrokers.

Basically, I suppose, it was a further expression of the unrivalled passion of the Hong Kong Chinese for gambling—a passion that makes horse-racing an obsession and fills every night in the city with the non-stop click-clacking of mah-jong pieces being moved around on countless game tables. Perhaps, too, it had its roots in the *hui*, an ancient Chinese folk institution that came into being a millennium before the first joint stock company was floated in Europe. A *hui* (literally "association") was a group of Chinese who banded together to lend money and to trade. Eventually it came also to function as a kind of mutual savings club, allowing each member in turn to borrow the *hui's* total monthly subscriptions for personal investment—at a high rate of interest. As long as members could repay the money, the *hui* was successful, but the risks were often high.

Huis were certainly a factor in the 1972 Stock Market Stampede. Most of the plungers had not the faintest notion that a share certificate represented a holding in a business. The stock market was just the most glorious and most remunerative game of chance ever invented. And for 15

A hawker of colour slides barters with a tourist in Tiger Balm Gardens, situated above Causeway Bay. The gardens, including a maze of colourfully painted concrete, were built by a Chinese family that amassed a fortune from sales of a panacea ointment, from which the tourist attraction got its name.

JAN MICHAEL JOBANEK

unforgettable months—as the Hang Seng Index, Hong Kong's equivalent of America's Dow-Jones and Britain's *Financial Times* Index, rocketed from 346.81 to an all-time high of 1774.96 in March, 1973—it seemed that *every* player must be a winner.

I shall never forget the scenes on Ice House Street, Hong Kong's Wall Street, so named because it once had a storehouse for ice which was brought from northern China in the winter for sale in the summer. The crowds gawking at the stock quotations posted in brokers' windows were so thick that they blocked traffic. They were made up of secretaries and amahs, coolies and horn-rimmed junior executives, hairdressers and errand boys. All had a few dollars going for them and believed they couldn't lose. A chartered accountant, musing aloud on the irrepressible optimism of the Chinese, said: "You can incorporate anything, anything at all. I could incorporate my dog, and the issue would be oversubscribed the first day. A week later, it would be selling for ten times the par value."

He was not exaggerating. There were some Hong Kong companies that had no assets at all beyond their stationery and their share certificates. Among companies that did possess some concrete assets was one whose only property was a 16-year-old freighter held on a six-year lease. Its initial offering was over-subscribed threefold. A rival company, whose sole asset was a 25-year-old freighter on a two-year lease, fared even better. That corporation's initial issue was oversubscribed fivefold. A shipping line executive commented: "It's bound to make money—if the vessel can stay afloat. But that seems rather doubtful."

The stock market mania was not confined exclusively to the people of this money-mad metropolis. Hong Kong had for a long time been an attractive refuge for money from questionable sources because controls on non-sterling currency movement were virtually non-existent. As a result, hot—or, to say the least, very warm—money poured in from sources all over Asia, and some big operators, who should have known better, were caught up in the general craziness. The wonder, however, was not that the fever spread so far and wide, but that it lasted so long.

The bubble burst on "Black Tuesday", March 20, 1973. That day the Hang Seng dipped 105.61 points. A few days later it plunged 188.7 points. Unfortunately, Eric Ho Tung had been abroad when the fever caught hold, and in his absence I, too, had played with the fire. When he returned a few months later, he told me to sell immediately, even though it entailed a 30 per cent loss. I did so, in spite of the pain. Meanwhile, the great majority of investors hung on, ever optimistic that the market would soon recover. It didn't. By November, 1974, the Hang Seng had fallen below 200—more than 1,574 points down from its peak—and thousands of Hong Kong residents were ruined. It should presumably have reduced Hong Kong to the kind of suicidal despair associated with the Wall Street crash of 1929. Indeed, there were a few suicides. But, in general, the money-minded people of Hong Kong are never easily discouraged from gambling. A few years later, when the index began to rise again, most of the earlier victims came back into the market, convinced all over again that they couldn't lose.

It was only natural. After all, most of Hong Kong's residents spring from a culture that sees life as an endless wheel of fortune spinning anew from year to year. "Kung Hei Fat Choy", they say at each fresh turn of the wheel —"Rejoice and grow rich". And the finest, most sincere compliment one can make to a Chinese acquaintance of any time is: Kung Hei Fat Fuk (Congratulations, I see you've put on prosperity). But the people of Hong Kong cannot wait patiently for opportunities to prosper. They must strive and work, ever aware that their time is limited by the expiration of the lease of the New Territories in 1997. And they must remain ever alert to the violent political and economic disruptions that their resilience—and, undeniably, their luck—have enabled them to exploit in the past.

"Made in Hong Kong"

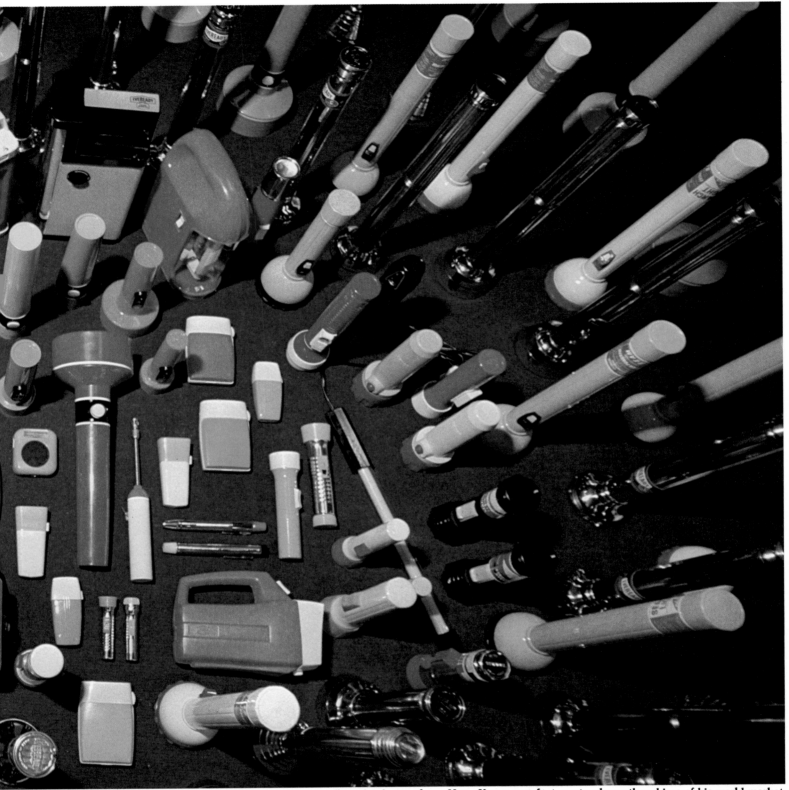

Scores of battery-operated lights in many sizes and colours reflect the desire of one Hong Kong manufacturer to please the whims of his world market.

In a sustained burst of manufacturing growth that began in the 1950s, Hong Kong transformed itself from a port that traded mainly in other people's goods into a producer making two thirds of everything it sells abroad. Flooding the globe with clothing and small appliances, toys and computer components, the tiny Colony competed so successfully for markets that it was soon being counted with the world's top exporting nations.

Where less bold manufacturers drew the line, Hong Kong's adventurous entrepreneurs drew a blueprint, risking large sums of money on innovative ideas ranging from dolls that "give birth" to sophisticated electronic devices. Backed by an industrious and adaptable labour force, the nerve and ingenuity of the Colony's capitalists made the words "Made in Hong Kong" one of the most familiar labels in the world.

Looking as much like riveters as rug makers, workers in a carpet factory knot threads on to fabric backing with electric tools to form traditional patterns.

Mechanizing an Ancient Skill

Old ways of Chinese carpet-making—individual families working with secret techniques and spending years to create one, unique rug—have been shattered in Hong Kong. Here, assembly line workers use ingeniously designed power tools that dramatically reduce the time required by old methods. The carpets, turned out by the thousands, may not appeal to collectors, but good quality and relatively low price assure a ready worldwide market.

By using electric clippers, a skilled carpet-factory worker is able to make a quick but nonetheless meticulous job of contouring the nap on a deep-pile rug.

Stacked in bundles, pieces of denim already cut to jeans shape wait to be sewn in a Hong Kong factory.

Big Boom in Blue Jeans

Partly because of a global mania for denim clothing, to which Hong Kong eagerly responded, the garment industry has led the Colony's economic boom. By the mid-1970s Hong Kong had become the world's foremost exporter of apparel, and more than half its work-force was employed making textiles and clothing. A factory like the one on these pages may employ up to 2,500 workers and handle $25 million worth of business a year.

As evidence of her productivity, a seamstress is nearly buried by a pile of jeans she has sewn. The factory she works in turns out seven million pairs annually.

An electric fan speeds up the drying time of floral still-lifes and a flotilla of nearly identical clipper ships painted on canvases of varying dimensions.

Art from Assembly Lines

Hong Kong's businessmen have a gift for detecting a hole in the market and filling it. For the many customers around the world who prefer art "originals" to mechanical reproductions, this workshop mass-produces oils on canvas. Specialists in ships, flowers or landscapes work on the same scene again and again, each completing as many as a hundred pictures a week. Often 2,000 copies of a single design are sold abroad.

Amid half-finished pictures left to dry before other colours are added, painters add their contributions to subjects they know well from constant repetition.

From father to tiniest child, this family form an assembly line, putting together and packaging plastic toys.

A Toll Exacted from the Young

The toy business is a natural arena for fast-moving manufacturers of the kind abounding in Hong Kong—men who can seize a new idea, exploit it and drop it before it is outdated. But the Colony's success as a producer and exporter of toys sometimes exacts a human price. Some of the work is contracted out to families who, desperate to maintain a standard of living, compel even their small children to work long hours assembling the toys.

Children assembling construction kits that American and European youngsters will eventually play with, tackle a daunting mound of components.

4

Men, Gods and Spirits

Eighteen months before we left Hong Kong, a dignified Chinese called at our home. He was solemnly impressive and he conducted himself like a medical specialist called in to consult on a particularly puzzling illness. Only the absence of a doctor's black bag made this image incomplete. He carried instead a large, circular device that resembled a box-compass. Its magnetic needle was free to rotate on a horizontal dial, but the dial did not show directional points; it was marked with the 12 signs of the Chinese zodiac and other esoteric symbols.

My wife and I were tense. Earlier we had talked almost light-heartedly about the idea of inviting a *feng shui* man into the house. It was very different now that the professional soothsayer was seated in our living room and so seriously preparing to look into our futures. What would he see? Did we really want to know?

For several minutes he studied our faces intently by the technique known as *Kan-hsiang*—spying out fate by reading the countenance. Then, after determining our birth dates in the Chinese calendar, he started to work out our horoscopes, all the time referring to his astrological tables. Finally he made a pronouncement: "You are planning major changes in your lives, a long journey and a change of residence. By all means, plan. It will not happen this year, but the next. Still, there is more to fear from indecision than from hasty action." (He was correct. We were indeed planning a long journey and change of residence; and, true enough, it did not happen until half-way through the following year.)

The *feng shui* man now examined all our fortunes individually. Our children were at school in England; but, given their dates and times of birth, he discussed their future in terms so relevant one would have imagined that he knew them intimately. In general, he saw almost un-adulterated good fortune ahead. However, it was his mission to ensure that the good fortune was not thwarted by his clients' own carelessness. He therefore made a tour of the house, looking for any physical features that might disturb the invisible spirits in our vicinity.

We hung upon his deliberations. Not long before, a neighbour of ours had called in a *feng shui* man because his wife was suffering a persistent abdominal pain the doctors could not diagnose. The consultant told her to move her bed to bring it into proper alignment with the path of the spirits that roamed Shouson Hill Road. Soon afterwards the pain disappeared. Now my wife followed our *feng shui* man through our rooms, fearful that he would order a major shift of furniture in our cramped quarters. But we were

On a Chinese grave in Hong Kong, a lavish array of food, including a whole roast pig, has been laid out as an offering to the spirit of the dead. The woman kowtowing at the family graveside is one of thousands of Chinese who flock to the cemeteries during the spring festival of Ching Ming to reaffirm their close communion with the world of their ancestors.

lucky. He directed only one change: a slight re-positioning of my wife's vanity table so that the mirror would not face the bedroom door and drive benevolent spirits away. (How stupid of us not to have spotted that necessity for ourselves.) He also suggested that the door be left ajar to avoid trapping malignant spirits. This done, our good fortune was guaranteed.

For us this encounter was a novel experience, but very few Chinese "belongers" would dream of making an important decision without consulting a *feng shui* man or similar figure. The fortune-teller is a kind of secular priest. He is also father confessor, psychiatrist, adviser to the love-lorn, and a reassuring family doctor. Most Hong Kong Chinese, from amahs to tycoons, have their favourite seer. Many will drop in on him even when they have no major decision to make—just as they might visit the doctor for a routine check-up.

Hong Kong's respect for the powers of the *feng shui* man highlights one aspect of the city that makes living here such a fascinating experience. Its people openly espouse many ancient Chinese myths and religious customs that the authorities in the People's Republic of China are seeking to eradicate. Aggressively anti-superstitious Communists, for example, have all but done away with the open practice of *feng shui* in China itself. To most Maoists, soothsaying seems like so much mumbo-jumbo, just as it does to sceptical Western minds. But belief in supernatural beings is still an integral part of life in the Colony, which is a living repository of traditional Chinese culture.

At times Hong Kong's Chinese may appear to worship only money, but they in fact embrace an eclectic theology that has been developed over thousands of years. This amorphous faith, which transcends the narrow definitions imposed upon religion in the West, keeps them in a state of intimate communion with the spirits of their ancestors, and through those spirits, with countless gods, ghosts, and demons who inhabit not only numerous heavens and hells but also the earth. For this reason the Hong Kong year is punctuated with festivals that celebrate the influence of gods and spirits over the lives of men. In Communist China one of these festivals has been replaced by a holiday honouring the coming of spring, and all others are officially ignored—which means no one is given time off work to celebrate them. But the Chinese of Hong Kong cling tenaciously to the old observances—although, in some instances, they have modernized the manner in which they observe them. And, with similar tenacity, they continue to believe in the *feng shui* man.

One soothsayer I met in Hong Kong exercised almost dictatorial powers over his clientele—even though he was blind. Portentously called Golden Seven, he operated from an imaginatively decorated salon in a lower-middle-class section of Kowloon. A great lithograph of the Buddha covered an entire wall of his dimly lit consulting room. Incense sticks and red

A feng shui man, or geomancer, is reflected in the mirror of his consulting room as he uses a magnifying glass to read the palm of a client. Feng shui men continue to play an influential role in the life of Hong Kong's Chinese, dispensing advice on subjects ranging from business matters to affairs of the heart.

candles burned before the shrine among offerings of fruit and rice. Diffused light glowed from hanging lamps on which gaudy dragons perpetually chased their tails—an effect achieved by inner cylinders revolving in the convected heat of incandescent bulbs. In this awe-inspiring setting, Golden Seven sat behind a carved ebony table—a tall, thin Chinese with inch-long fingernails and eyes concealed behind dark glasses. The eyes looked inwards. His clients were convinced that, because this seer was blind to the deceptive, outward semblances of the material world, he was all the better equipped to discern the true realities of the esoteric spirit world that determine men's fate.

Golden Seven was highly esteemed for his ability to read the will of fate in order to advise others about how to arrange their lives—and make their fortunes. Why, then, did he not abandon his practice and turn his knowledge of the future to his own advantage? The answer to that obvious question, posed by sceptics and non-believers, came readily to our ever-practical Chinese friends. They did not offer the faintly metaphysical and slightly unsatisfactory rationalization that a soothsayer can only help others, not himself, by his occult powers. Their answer, infused with cheerful Chinese cynicism, was totally realistic: "I wouldn't call him dumb or unsuccessful. Golden Seven makes a very good living, sometimes several hundred dollars a day. Do you think that's bad for a blind man who has no technical or professional skills?"

The healthy cynicism of his devotees in no way inhibited their paying scrupulous attention to Golden Seven's predictions and faithfully obeying his instructions. I know a manufacturer who was told by the seer he should confess to his wife that he had been keeping a mistress but was now giving her up. He promptly did so.

"Yes, I know," the wife blandly replied. "Golden Seven told me a year ago you had a mistress—and that you would give her up within a year."

Such direct interference does not occur every day. Nevertheless, most of Golden Seven's clients would take equally drastic action on his advice. After all, everyone in Hong Kong knows about the illiterate and rather simple-minded amah who, by slavishly following Golden Seven's advice, ran a $180 investment on the stock exchange up to $36,000.

A Chinese editor I had known for years impressed me as being a thoroughly modern man. He was progressive in outlook and spoke bitterly against the superstition of his compatriots and contemptuously of the exaggerated claims made for traditional Chinese culture by both Chinese and foreign *aficionados*. Yet, one day this same man appeared with his abundantly trendy locks shorn into a brush-cut that would have seemed brutally short even on an army recruit. Without any embarrassment, he explained: "Golden Seven told me that I'd change my luck by cutting my hair. And he was right! Two days after the haircut, I was offered a great new job—and a good contract for a book. He knows his stuff."

On the birthday of Tin Hau, the goddess of
seafarers, two gaily decorated junks carry
revellers to the big celebration held each year
at Joss House Bay. Along the way, the
passengers scatter symbolic "paper money"
to appease the spirits of the sea, and on
arrival they will join in elaborate dances and
traditional rites at the main Tin Hau temple.

After 18 months, the editor's hair had finally returned to its original length. But his luck had turned sour. The magazine that employed him went out of business and he wasn't paid for the book.

"Well?" I asked. "What now? Another scalping?"

"I don't know," he confessed sheepishly. "I haven't got up the nerve to see Golden Seven again. It can't be just another hair-cut this time. But you've got to admit he was right the first time."

In spite of such cases of self-deception, I—like many other European belongers constantly exposed to the superstitions of Hong Kong's Chinese —eventually found it harder not to believe at all than to believe a little. Personal experiences at times strained my ability to account them to mere coincidence. I found my scepticism shaken when we celebrated our last Chinese New Year as Colony residents.

Twelve beasts (among them, the snake, the rat and the dog) lend their names and attributes to the years of the Chinese calendar in a cycle that has repeated itself for millennia. The New Year's Day preceding our departure most propitiously welcomed the Year of the Dragon—and better still, it was the Year of the Benevolent Dragon, the successor to the Malevolent Dragon who had initiated the previous 12-year cycle that brought many calamities to the world. Since our planned departure from Hong Kong was beginning a new cycle in our lives, we were especially interested in the portents. And in my case there were still more compelling reasons for taking such interest: I was born in the Year of the Dragon, so that the dragon is my personal totem. Also, quite fortuitously, I happened to be completing a long novel about a Hong Kong Eurasian family whose name meant West-Dragon and who had taken the dragon as their symbol.

The auguries, we learned, were splendid. I was, therefore, delighted but not astonished when my closest Chinese friend called to tell me that, partly because of my help, his mother in Shanghai was being allowed by the Communists to come to Hong Kong. I had asked the Hong Kong Immigration Department to write to the Shanghai authorities affirming that Mrs. Yen would indeed be permitted to stay in the Colony—contrary to what she had been told by her local Security Bureau. But it seemed more than coincidental that she had finally received her exit visa after exactly 12 years of striving for it.

Any vestigial scepticism I had regarding the auspiciousness for me of the Year of the Dragon was dissolved when I met Mrs. Yen for the first time. Concealed under the clothing in her suitcase was a present she had brought for my wife—a gift we treasure so highly that it now hangs in the entrance of our house in Ireland. An embroidered black-silk rectangle, exquisitely worked a century ago, it depicts two dragons facing each other. Mrs. Yen had not known that I was a child of the dragon.

When we flew out of Kai Tak Airport in Kowloon (Kowloon means Nine Dragons), most of the small gifts from our friends traditional on parting

At a funeral ceremony held by a Hakka family, the mourners have gathered in a bamboo shelter built for the occasion near the home of the deceased. They are watching two priests enact the eventual passage to Heaven of the dead person's spirit. During the ceremony, gifts are burned and prayers offered to help the spirit on its journey.

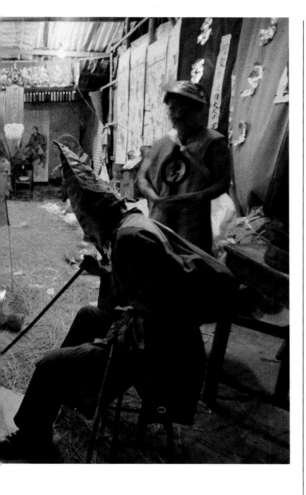

were also dragons—among them a jade dragon buckle and a cylindrical, ivory powder-box carved with *bas relief* dragons. We could, thereafter, hardly do less than rename our house in Ireland "Loongshan" (Dragon Mountain) or fail to have our stationery engraved with a dragon.

The innate faith of the Hong Kong Chinese in man's ability to read the will of Heaven—and to use it to his own ends—has given them a pragmatic approach to religion, which is not to say that they are disrespectful of their gods and ancestors or negligent in their veneration of them. Every household has its ancestral shrine. Shops offer a selection of images of hundreds of divinities, and ancient rites in connection with birth, marriage and death are still widely observed.

But to understand just how practical the Colony's Chinese are in the practice of their religion, let us consider for a moment the Grandfather's Bones Jar. When I first came to Hong Kong, a favourite adornment of non-Chinese households was a pottery jar, two-and-a-half feet high and with a rough-glazed brown finish. Such jars were used as vases or lamp bases. Similar jars banked the outlying hillsides of the New Territories. Each of them, I was to learn, contained the polished bones of someone's grandfather or grandmother. Sombrely elegant, the jars are normally crowned by hemispherical lids on which rest stones and slips of paper—"spirit money" intended to provide for the comfort of the departed in the other world.

The use by my friends of such ancestral urns for cosy, domestic purposes was perhaps macabre, if not downright disrespectful. Yet, significantly, the Chinese saw no particular incongruity in foreigners adapting them to such mundane uses because they themselves are so essentially practical as well as highly religious. The use to which the Chinese themselves put the Grandfather's Bones Jar—which they call a Golden Pagoda—is a vivid example of their practicality and religiosity working in unison.

As I mentioned earlier, Hong Kong is so irremediably short of land that a man of property—such as ex-gravedigger Mr. Chow Yao—can obtain as much as $60,000 for the freehold of a choice six-by-three grave site. Even the cheapest of permanent plots is far beyond the pocket of the vast majority of Hong Kong "belongers". At the same time, the Chinese *know* beyond doubt that their own welfare, as well as the peace of their ancestors, requires them to honour the relics of the departed in a manner as close as possible to the traditional rites prescribed by the sage Confucius. Their usual solution, therefore, is a compromise: renting a grave for a six-year tenure and having the bones exhumed and carefully cleaned, then placed in a Golden Pagoda.

Today these ancestor jars are most often seen where a steep hillside overlooks a running stream or the sea. That juxtaposition of terrain— fortunately common in the Colony—virtually guarantees good fortune and protection from evil spirits. At least, so says the *feng shui* man, who is the master of the science of "reading" fate in the winds and waters, as well as the land. He is reputedly in intimate communication with all the myriad spirits, ghosts, gods and demons that inhabit the earth, and his services are therefore crucial when it comes to positioning urns and graves.

Thus laid properly to rest, the dead become a focal point for the living. At the Ching Ming (Bright and Clear) festival, which approximately co-incides with Easter, hundreds of thousands of Hong Kong Chinese make pilgrimages to graves or urns where they offer flowers and food to the spirits of the departed. The ritual is accompanied by a display of exhilaration and levity which, to uninitiated Westerners, might seem more suited to a football stadium than to a cemetery. But then there is, and can be, no overwhelming grief because to Hong Kong's Chinese, the dead and the living are indivisible. A carefree picnic among the bone jars is not irreverent, but a normal occasion for pleasure.

During Ching Ming, people dig up graves of ancestors who have been buried long enough for decomposition to have occurred. Colonel Valentine Burkhardt, already well into his seventies when we were his neighbours in Stanley, gave an admirable, matter-of-fact description of this process in his charming compilation called *Chinese Creeds and Customs*: "The whole family . . . repairs to the cemetery. . . . The valuables contained in the coffin are first removed and revert to the family. If there is a grandson available, the skull is handed to him to hold while the bones are being removed. Great care is taken in assembling the skeleton. The large bones are easily identifiable, but the small ones in the hands and feet might get mixed, so they are separated out and, after cleaning, are wrapped in paper and labelled. The cleansing is now done with sandpaper, though originally sand alone was used as an abrasive. The packing of the urn is entrusted to the undertaker, who arranges the contents in the natural order with the skull on top."

The practice may appear grisly to Westerners. I myself still find it so. But the Colony's Chinese are accustomed to adapting to necessity and, besides, they do not view death in quite the same manner as do many other peoples. This may sound like a repetition of the old fallacy with which Westerners making violent intrusions into Asia have so long comforted themselves. The cliché goes: "Orientals are careless of human life; individual existence doesn't mean as much to them as to us." I know this not to be true.

The Chinese is just as concerned about preserving his own life as anyone else. And he is just as concerned about the lives of others—when circumstances allow him that luxury. But he does not regard a funeral or a visit to his ancestors' urns as a primarily doleful occasion. That's because he sees the life of mankind as an unbroken continuum of the dead, the living and yet unborn; by paying homage to the spirits of his ancestors he reaffirms the eternal life of mankind, honouring both himself and his descendants. Grave-visiting is therefore an occasion for joy as well as sorrow.

At a hillside cemetery on the island of Cheung Chau, relatives celebrate Ching Ming by laying out food offerings and joss sticks in front of the gravestones.

Caring for the Dead

For many of Hong Kong's Chinese, visiting the graves of kinsfolk is affirmation of the invisible bond between the living and the dead. Never is this belief more evident than at the annual spring festival of Ching Ming (which literally means "Bright and Clear"). Relatives of the dead flock to the Colony's cemeteries to offer gifts to the souls of the departed and to sweep their graves. People who cannot continue to pay the rent for a large burial place in crowded Hong Kong may perform the additional ritual of unearthing the loved one's skeleton. Bones are cleaned and polished, then stacked in an urn in precise and ascending order from feet to skull. The urn may then be reburied in a smaller and less costly space, or taken home to be revered in a family shrine.

While a gravedigger hurriedly completes a grave, a bereaved family attired in traditional white mourning robes gather in front of a ceremonial fire to pray.

A disjointed skeleton removed from the ground lies sprawled on a sheet of paper prior to being washed, sandpapered and placed in an earthenware burial urn.

Bones that have been gently cleaned are sorted out for reburial in an urn.

Sticks of incense burn beside an open trench where urns wait to be interred.

Many Hong Kong Chinese, including some supposedly devout adherents of Communist materialism, were therefore dismayed when China's Prime Minister, Chou En-lai, ordered his ashes scattered when he died. The shrewd ones recognized that, his astuteness reaching beyond the bourne of life, he was simultaneously demonstrating his own liberation from traditional superstition and ensuring that his remains would not become a shuttlecock in future factional disputes. But Confucian doctrine holds that a man's body, as a sacred gift from his ancestors, must be returned to them entire and unblemished.

Another occasion for sprucing up graves and polishing ancestral bones falls in the autumn during the festival called Chung Yeung or the Double Ninth because it is held on the ninth day of the ninth moon by the lunar calendar. On this day, too, countless thousands of worshippers in holiday dress and mood make their way up Victoria Peak or climb the hills of the New Territories to renew their own claims upon good fortune. It is a traditional journey in remembrance of a certain Huan Ching who, some 2,000 years ago, faithfully accepted the advice of a soothsayer and fled with his family to a high mountaintop in China. On his return, it is said, he found that all those who had remained behind in his village had been killed on the Double Ninth by a catastrophe—a sudden flood, typhoon, earthquake or epidemic, depending on which version of the legend one accepts. Nowadays, many Hong Kong Chinese who climb to high places on this day (or, more conveniently, ride express lifts to the top of new skyscrapers) are only vaguely aware of the origin of the custom. But they are all determined to "elevate their luck" by attaining heights.

The legend of the virtuous man who escaped natural disaster is, of course, reminiscent of Lot's departure from the doomed cities of Sodom and Gomorrah or Noah's deliverance after God had enjoined him to build the Ark. Like almost all the world's mythologies, Chinese mythology displays remarkable parallels to the Judaeo-Christian Bible—or, if one prefers, the Bible displays close parallels to various mythologies. In Chinese legend the nearest equivalent to Noah is the Great Yü, who lived more than four thousand years ago when primordial floods, lapping the highest mountain peaks, threatened mankind. But there is one essential difference between his escape and that of Noah. The Great Yü did not simply obey the instructions of Heaven to save himself, his family and the different species of animals by waiting for the waters to recede. Rather, he took Heaven and earth by the forelock and preserved the lives of all mankind by building a series of gigantic dams.

Today enormous dikes of wicker, stone and packed earth still supplement modern dams to contain and channel the great rivers of the Chengtu Basin in Szechwan, the most fertile and populous province of China. These may truly be the dams built by the Great Yü, his original handiwork having been constantly refurbished by the industry of his des-

Its branches trussed with pink ribbons, a peach tree that has been grown in a nursery in the New Territories awaits delivery to a Hong Kong family for the New Year celebrations. The blossoms it will put forth in the coming month are believed to bring good fortune.

cendants. In this way, to the Chinese mind, the seamless, unbreakable continuity of mankind comprehends not only the bodies and spirits of men, but also their material creations.

As a reward for the Great Yü's labours, the emperor named him successor to the throne. Eventually the Great Yü became a divinity—one among hundreds of those deified over the millennia by the gradual process of mythological evolution and now worshipped at Hong Kong's 600 Taoist and Buddhist shrines. It is usually the women—and, most often, older women—who visit the temples to speak to these gods. But the men are also believers, even if their approach is less reverential. Like the ancient Greeks, Hong Kong's Chinese bribe, cajole and bully their many gods, rewarding them for favours received and wreaking retribution upon them for any calamities that occur.

My favourite example of this attitude is the treatment of Tsao Kwan, a deity enshrined in every Chinese household as the Kitchen God. Some families keep small carved figures of Tsao Kwan in their kitchens; others content themselves with a shiny lithograph or a wooden plaque inscribed with felicitous prayers. Before that shrine, at every festival, they burn incense and lay out offerings such as crisp pork, baked duck and boiled chicken. Yet Tsao Kwan, one of the best-loved gods in the Chinese pantheon, is also one of the most abused.

The Kitchen God's supreme glorification—and his corruption—occurs at the Chinese New Year, which can fall anywhere from late January to late February. According to popular belief, this god spends each year here on earth compiling a comprehensive dossier on every family's activities and behaviour. At the Lunar New Year he has seven days' to report back to his superiors in Heaven. The nature of his report determines whether a family enjoys good luck or is visited by misfortune during the year to come.

That function, of course, gives Tsao Kwan a very powerful position. True to Hong Kong's mores, every household is prepared to resort to unashamed bribery to ensure that the god will say only sweet things. Tsao Kwan is offered sugar cane and brown sugar to fortify him for his journey back to Heaven. Some householders go further. They smear the figure's lips with honey or sugar-water in hopes of pleasing him and, simultaneously, sealing his mouth with the sticky substances in order to prevent unfavourable accounting. Although it is not considered quite sporting, an even more drastic device is employed to influence the god's report: some families, either hyper-cautious or deservedly apprehensive, will actually ply the Kitchen God with opium. A dollop of the sticky, brown-black narcotic, applied to the god's lips or burned before his image, is calculated to reduce him to such a euphorically befuddled state that his reports are either overwhelmingly favourable or, at worst, totally unintelligible. A god needs to be resilient to work for a canny Hong Kong Chinese clan who want only the best for themselves in the coming year.

"Originally the Chinese New Year was a most unlucky day," explained a matron from Shanghai, a devout Roman Catholic who also religiously observed the old Chinese festivals. "To ward off ill-luck, people set off firecrackers and bathed with special waters boiled with medicinal leaves to draw out all the evil in them. The lights remained lit throughout the night, while brooms that could brush aside good fortune and knives that could cause injury were carefully hidden away before midnight. Many old-fashioned people still do not sweep their floors on New Year's Day for fear of sweeping out the good luck promised them during the coming year."

Most of the people of Hong Kong are no longer consciously aware of that symbolic transition from evil to good. Yet they unconsciously affirm it in their own behaviour. All debts should be settled before the New Year, and all quarrels should be reconciled so that men may greet the new cycle of the earth with a conscience as clean as the new clothes everyone dons on New Year's Eve. Prodigies of scrubbing, dusting and polishing serve the same purpose. The annual ritual is reminiscent of spring cleaning or, among Jewish families, the meticulous preparations for Passover. All this cleansing is motivated by the instinctive urge to renew all things in the household, just as earth renews itself in the spring, the time of blossoming and birth.

To Hong Kong Chinese, the Lunar New Year is a combination of Christmas, Thanksgiving, Easter, Mardi Gras and the Fourth of July or Guy Fawkes' Day. The holiday's hold on all Chinese people remains so strong that it is, after being proscribed for years, once again celebrated in the People's Republic, where they have modest feasts and shops become selectively colourful with new consumer goods hoarded by the authorities against the day. Peking, however, celebrates the "Spring Festival", rather than the "New Year" since the lunar calendar has been abolished.

Hong Kong itself celebrates the New Year with uninhibited gaiety. Adults await the festival with almost as much anticipation as the wildly eager children, and the spirit of joy that bubbles in the streets at this time is one of the aspects of the Colony that I now miss most. The servants of Chinese families remain on duty to receive the obligatory gifts from their employers' friends; and the staffs of restaurants, clubs and hotels work harder than at any other time of the year, their minds on the bonuses to come. Otherwise, there is no nonsense about a mere two-day holiday; most Hong Kong workers take at least three or four days off, while many stretch it to five or six days. The period is dreaded by many foreign housewives who are used to the service of amahs and daunted by their primitive kitchens, which, because the servants prefer their own utensils, have few Western appliances. Those who cannot bear the prospect of not being attended to or the unending noise of celebration may seek refuge in one of the big hotels that offer special New Year rates. But long-settled foreigners tend to look forward to this festival just as eagerly as their Chinese friends.

Beneath giant, suspended coils of incense, the ornate altar at Man Mo Temple blazes with joss sticks lit to honour Buddhist deities. Hong Kong is dotted with more than a thousand temples for the Colony's adherents of Buddhism, Taoism and various folk religions.

The preparations begin with the purchase of so many miniature orange trees, peach blossoms—just starting to bloom at this time of the year—and other flowers that it seems the sparse forests of the New Territories are being moved *en bloc* to Kowloon and Hong Kong Island on the roofs of private cars or in lorries. Most prominent are the pink-flowered branches of peach trees—or, for the more affluent, entire peach trees. By driving into the New Territories I found that I could buy a small cut peach tree for a third of what it would have cost at a downtown florist. I was pleased to find that the inborn Chinese instinct for conservation was effectively preventing the denuding of the area. An amiable, hunch-backed gardener showed me the permanent tree stocks on which the New Year's trees are grown and he told me that it took two years to grow a moderate-size tree (say, three-foot-high) or as long as 10 years for a nine-foot-high grandfather tree which might sell at $2,000 or more.

White flowers called "hanging bells" are another favourite New Year decoration, although some particularly superstitious people will not permit those delicate blooms, each like a tiny enamelled thimble, in their houses. In Chinese, as in English, the word "hang" has two meanings, and the prudent would no more welcome those floral harbingers of ill-fortune than they would discuss rope in the home of a hanged man. Instead, they disperse pots of miniature oranges which are certain to bring good luck. One variety is the small, tart citrus fruit called a kumquat, an English adaptation of the Cantonese name *gamkwut*, meaning golden orange. The second variety—elongated, pulpy and bitter—is esteemed even though it is inedible. It is called *saikwok* (lucky fruit).

The Chinese passion for food, springing perhaps from ancient memories of famine, flourishes most exuberantly in Hong Kong at the New Year. Householders offer visitors eight varieties of candied fruit in lacquered or enamelled containers designed for that purpose. Among the delicacies that turn up at this time of year is preserved lotus stalk. I shall never forget its bitter-sweet tang. To think of lotus stalks now is to yearn for dozens of the *chiao-tze*—plump dumplings symbolizing long life and renewal—that invariably follow. *Chiao-tze* were originally brought to Hong Kong from the north, but they are now avidly devoured by the Cantonese.

As the New Year approaches, the streets of Hong Kong are filled with eager shoppers in their tens of thousands. Above all, the New Year's Fair in Victoria Park is crowded with bargain hunters who wait until the last possible moment to make their purchases from stall-owners eager to dispose of their remaining stock. On our last New Year's Eve in Hong Kong, my wife and I set out with friends on a sentimental visit to that fair, which had always delighted our children. We could not get within a mile of the acetylene-lit park: the surrounding streets were solid streams of slow-moving automobiles and the sidewalks and roads were thronged with revellers munching on melon seeds and candied fruit.

In Aberdeen harbour, oarsmen prepare to launch their boat before fixing the dragon's head to the prow.

The Fury of the Race

Early summer is the time of the Dragon Boat Festival, when for a day the people of Hong Kong abandon their work and crowd into ports and fishing villages along the Colony's coasts to watch one of the noisiest and oldest regattas in the world. (The first dragon boat race is said to have taken place some 2,300 years ago.) At each venue, to the accompaniment of cymbals and big drums, amateur crews of up to 70 oarsmen race each other in dragon boats that are as slim as panatellas and as long as 125 feet. Each craft is adorned with the wooden head of a dragon, an influential beast in Chinese folklore: legend has it that if replica dragons compete on earth, those in the sky will be spurred into battle, producing thunder and causing harvest-ensuring summer rains to fall.

A Regatta for Dragons

In the main dragon races—held at Yaumati, Tai Po, Stanley, or at Aberdeen (where these pictures were taken)—as many as 35 teams may be entered. They come from fishing communities, organized groups such as the police, sports clubs or cargo vessel associations. In each heat, two or three boats compete over an 800-yard course. The crews' furious paddling throws up billows of spray, and since—dragons or no dragons—the summer rains break around this time of year, the competitors often end up drenched. That is a small price to pay for the chance to gain the prestige accorded the victors.

Lining up for the start is tricky, because at slow speed the boats are unstable.

Once the race is under way, the paddlers pace their strokes to the beat of drums mounted amidships and respond to the urgings of their on-board coaches.

One of several women-only teams that have entered the dragon races in recent years show their delight as they cross the finishing line, first in their heat.

From the crowd, murmuring like the sea lapping the shore, came a low, reiterated sound as the revellers greeted each other with the prescribed New Year's formula: *Kung Hei Fat Choy* (Rejoice and Grow Rich.). Even in its most chaotic revels, avidly commercial Hong Kong never forgets its primary purpose. Invocations of prosperity are also expressed in gold characters hand-painted on red slips of paper that are the favourite New Year's decoration. The slips are posted on walls and doors wherever Chinese live or work. Holiday-makers can choose from a hundred or so slogans, most soliciting blessings from the God of Wealth and many praying for such rewards as "A Hall-full of Jade", "A Mass of Gold", or "Myriad Capital Increase". Others invoke blessings appropriate to the place where they are posted: on staircases, "Up and Down in Safety"; in offices, "May All Your Wishes Come True"; in living-rooms, "Young and Old Dwell in Harmony"; in classrooms, "All Examinations Passed with Honours". Some are just large single characters invoking "Prosperity", "Happiness" or "Longevity".

In recent years Hong Kong has seen the introduction of embossed plastic slips—anathema to purists, including myself. Nevertheless, it simply isn't the Chinese New Year without such gaudy invocations, no matter how they are produced, and many foreign residents have come to share this compulsion of Hong Kong's Chinese to propitiate and woo the fates. It is strange how that compulsion grows. I never have worried about hats on beds, black cats crossing my path, opening umbrellas in the house, or walking under ladders. But the beliefs (superstitions, if you wish) that surround the Chinese New Year have put roots deep into my subconscious. Even now, living in Ireland, my wife and I grow uneasy if we can't post those red slips at the appropriate time (fortunately, we took more than a hundred with us when we left Hong Kong). Our children, at school in England, feel exactly the same; they fret if they don't receive red slips to put up in their rooms, just as they are unhappy if they don't receive mooncakes for the autumnal Moon Festival.

The Chinese New Year is a very special experience for children. They stuff themselves on the seasonal abundance of savouries and sweets— sugar-coated lotus seeds, melon seeds, chocolate "coins" wrapped in gold foil—and gleefully count the money they are given in *lai see*, red packets containing banknotes. They are allowed the rare indulgence of staying up hours past their normal bedtimes. When they are finally tucked into bed—torpid, their appetites and guileless greed satiated—they have put the final seal upon this family holiday, giving their parents the same sort of vicarious pleasure that Western children give theirs at Christmas.

The *lai see* envelopes (the words literally mean "positive gain") are not for children only. They are also used for the obligatory additional month's pay given at the New Year to all domestic employees, from gardeners and amahs to cooks and Number One Boys, and for all the lesser tips distributed to others who have given service during the year. These un-mistakable red packets imprinted with the character for "good luck" are a major feature of the holiday for the practical Hong Kong Chinese, who believe that gifts should not only be given, but should very much be seen when given. At the same time, adults exchange presents that may be as small as bottles of cognac or as large as Rolls-Royces. There is certainly much "positive gain" at the New Year. And some alarming expenditure.

After joining in this most important of all celebrations, the non-Chinese "belonger" may well feel excluded from some of the other festivals in Hong Kong. He can scarcely share in such esoteric delights as graveyard picnics at Ching Ming. There is, however, one other spectacular festival in which *every* Hong Kong "belonger" can participate with equal enjoy-ment. That is the Dragon Boat Festival held on the "Double Fifth"—the fifth day of the fifth month of the Chinese calendar (*pages 111-4*).

In all my years in the Colony I found no more pleasant way of passing an afternoon than lolling in the cockpit of my sloop *Roland Sathya* sipping a cold gin and lime juice while watching the exuberant gaiety of the Dragon Boat oarsmen, 50 or more of them in each of the long, narrow vessels. These boat races may be the most colourful in the world; they are cer-tainly the noisiest. Firecrackers are let off intermittently around the course and at the centre of each craft a big drum beats out the stroke rate for the paddlers, who thrash the water at a frenetic pace.

There are several different stories explaining the origin of this regatta, for which each of the Colony's fishing communities keeps a special boat. My favourite version says that it pays homage to Chü Yüan, a folk-hero who has been dead for millennia. Chü Yüan was a famous poet and statesman in the 4th Century B.C., and legend has it that he drowned himself in the Tung-t'ing Lake in protest against the oppressive policies of the prince of the feudal state of Ch'u (modern Hunan). Since suicide is the most forceful reproach one Chinese can offer another, he hoped his sacrifice would induce the prince to mend his ways. It is not known whether Chü Yüan achieved that purpose, but it is recorded that fishermen recognized him as a martyr and raced out in great numbers to search for his body. They looked in vain. Finally they contented them-selves with casting packets of cooked rice into the river as offerings to ensure the welfare of Chü Yüan's troubled spirit by luring away any evil water-spirits. Some 2,300 years later that search is still commemorated by the Dragon Boat races, during which sweet rice-cakes wrapped in lotus leaves are tossed overboard.

Each festival in Hong Kong has its particular food, and one in parti-cular—the Full Moon (or Mid Autumn) Festival—is almost overwhelmed by its attendant delicacies. On this occasion (the fifteenth day of the eighth moon) each region of China produces its own variety of round mooncakes that mirror the harvest moon. In Hong Kong every one of those varieties is available, from the heavy, egg-studded chestnut purée of Shanghai to the lighter Cantonese cakes stuffed with sweet bean paste. All are consumed with artless gluttony while the orange-gold moon hangs low over the Colony's sinuous hills.

The consumption of mooncake commemorates an uprising that led to the overthrow of China's Mongol rulers in the 14th Century. History relates that the chief conspirators completed their plans for the revolt by passing messages hidden in round cakes. The signal for armed action was then given by the simultaneous lighting of lanterns in the eaves of pagodas throughout the country. This signal, too, is remembered on the night of the Full Moon Festival, when adults and children troop into the parks and hills carrying lanterns fashioned in an extraordinary range of fanciful shapes and sizes. Countless thousands of them shimmer in the Hong Kong dusk—lanterns in the shapes of birds and butterflies, fish and lobsters, dragons and lions, elephants and chariots, even automobiles and modern battle tanks.

But the lanterns I like best celebrate another, less important holiday held on the fourteenth day of the seventh moon. That holiday, evocatively called the Hungry Ghosts Festival, is like the West's celebration of All Hallows' E'en. The Hong Kong Chinese, practical as ever in their relations with the spirit world, know that even a ghost can drift through limbo yearning for sustenance. Accordingly, every August, to make sure that no occult being feels slighted or forgotten, Hong Kong throws a special party for all the ghosts of the departed and all the spirits of the earth, the waters and the skies. In temples and houses, people lay out food for family ghosts and burn imitation money and clothing as offerings. Particular gifts are prepared for those unfortunate ghosts without descendants to feed them.

After the invocations, the offerings, the incense and the prayers, a fleet of miniature "ghost ships"—each about two feet long—with candles glowing in their holds, sets sail across the inlets and bays of the water-borne Colony. As the hours pass the candles flicker and die, but there is still enough light to make out the prayer inscribed on a banner that is always hung on the mast of the rearmost boat. The words encapsulate the living spirit of the intensely practical and deeply reverential people of Hong Kong: *Hsun-feng Teh-li.* Temper the Winds and Gain Profits.

Buns for the Spirits

Under a bamboo shelter, nine-foot-high papier mâché images of three presiding gods glare out through the lamplight on the first evening of the festival.

For four days every spring, peaceful little Cheung Chau, one of Hong Kong's outlying fishing islands, explodes in colour and noise as *Ta Chiu*—the Spirit Placating Festival—begins. Westerners call it the Bun Festival because large round buns are stuck on to 60-foot-high bamboo structures, ostensibly to feed the souls of island people who were murdered by pirates in the distant past. But after the dead have eaten, the living get their chance: the celebration's climax is a wild scramble up the "bun mountains" to snatch and devour the buns, which are said to bring good luck. The festival began in the 19th Century when the hungry spirits of the pirates' victims were thought to be bringing misfortune to the community. *Ta Chiu's* rituals, parades and general joyousness have made it a major attraction for both tourists and Hong Kong residents.

A bun-maker puts good-luck mottoes on his wares.

The paper messenger awaits his ritual burning.

Priests perform complex rites of dedication on a "spirit ground" in front of the island's main temple.

A Strict Time-Table for Tradition

To propitiate the spirits, the festival must begin on time (Taoist priests determine the exact date by divination); and all the rituals must be rigidly observed. At midnight on the first day, priests call gods and spirits to the festival by ceremonially burning a paper horseman carrying an invitation, and from then on events proceed in a prescribed sequence. But even adherence to proper timing cannot suppress the jovial merry-making of the celebration.

A team of lion-dancers—an inevitable feature of Chinese festivals—amuse a crowd between processions by manipulating their cloth lion on top of a pole.

A little boy stands nonchalantly on an axe handle.

A big water-lily seems to hold a child in mid-air.

A doll-like girl rides on a frame hidden by her gown.

A child, seeming to carry another, gets a face wipe.

Children Who Float on Air

The second day brings one of the festival's most startling features: a procession in which solemn little children, as still as statues, appear to float above the crowds, precariously balanced on seemingly insubstantial supports. In reality they are securely harnessed to strong steel frameworks completely concealed beneath their fancy costumes. The islanders take great pride in showing off their children in these strange illusions of weightlessness.

Surrounded by a forest of silken banners, a girl perches on a tenuous column of objects, all ultimately resting on a toy pistol in another child's hand.

Joss sticks are lighted to scent the air as crowds await the bun scramble.

Ready for the Mad Rush

During the third day, excitement builds as the festival nears its climax: the moment when young men race up the "bun mountains" to grab all the buns they can. Exactly at midnight, after peering through an amber monocle to make sure that all the ghosts have finished eating, a priest gives the starting signal.

Early arrivals gather near the bamboo towers that are entirely covered with buns weighing nearly half a pound each. None is touched until the race begins.

Seconds after midnight, the bun mountains are aswarm with climbers.

Within minutes the young men have stripped most of the buns from the towers. When the last one is taken, the crowd goes home to continue merry-making.

5

An Infinitely Varied Cuisine

Pressed ducks, their glazed skins glinting beneath a bare bulb, hang in regimented rows inside a Hong Kong shop. The ducks have been salted, dabbed with ginger sauce and pepper, and then dried by exposing them to a winter breeze for 10 days—an example of the careful food preparation that makes Chinese cuisine among the most delicious in the world.

I once asked a scholar whose knowledge of the culture and psychology of Hong Kong's Chinese surpasses the encyclopaedic, what they liked most: sex, gambling or food? "That's a difficult question," he replied after pondering a while. "It's hard to say whether it's gambling or food."

He finally decided that eating—which to the Chinese is at once an art, a science and a great pleasure—takes precedence even over gambling. "Most people eat to live," my Chinese friends in Hong Kong are fond of saying, "but we live to eat." It is only natural that the Chinese should believe that they rather than the French, are the authors of that aphorism (just as Nikita Khrushchev once startled an American statesman with "the old Russian saying" that Moscow was not built in a day). After all, the Chinese have been pre-occupied with good eating for a very long time.

Some 2,500 years ago the venerated sage Confucius turned his philosophical attention to the subject, prescribing the proper foods, their correct preparation and the etiquette of their consumption. He told his followers to avoid rice injured by heat or dampness, "dried meat bought in the market", any food that was discoloured and any that was not in season. Rice should be "finely cleaned" and meat "cut quite small" (the latter requirement leading indirectly to the use of chopsticks). Moreover, the amount of meat eaten should not "exceed the due proportion for the rice". But Confucius set no limit on the amount of wine consumed at a meal, except that the diner should "not allow himself to be confused by it".

During the millennia since the rules were set forth, the Chinese developed the world's most varied cuisine—or, more accurately, cuisines, because the cooking generally described as "Chinese" covers a range of regional styles that differ as much from each other as does, say, English food from Russian. (The use of chopsticks is the only feature all have in common.) Culinary scholars sometimes disagree over the classifications but, broadly speaking, Chinese cooking can be divided into four major regional categories: southern, or Cantonese, cuisine—what most Europeans and Americans think of as "Chinese food" but which, on its home ground, is infinitely varied; northern cuisine—dominated by the food of the Peking region, and the Chinese style that is most like European cooking, partly because it depends for a staple more on wheat flour (noodles and dumplings) than on rice; eastern, or Shanghai, cuisine—which includes many seafood dishes from the coastal region; and western cuisine—mainly from Szechwan province and noted for its hot spices. Within these broad groupings there are at least a dozen distinct minor styles.

Thanks to refugees who brought their own taste and recipes from the People's Republic, all the major Chinese cuisines and most of their minor variations are now available in Hong Kong. I cannot begin to discuss adequately all of them, but I do hope to describe enough dishes I have eaten there and loved, to show why the Colony, once a gastronomic backwater, is now one of the world's premier resorts for gourmets.

Visitors to the Colony are not the only ones who delight their palates there. All classes of Hong Kong Chinese, from millionaire textile manufacturers to paddy farmers and domestic servants, share a common dedication to the pleasures of the table. The strength of that dedication was made particularly clear to me one evening in the late 1960s when my wife and I were entertaining an American motion picture producer.

The producer had flown to Hong Kong from Europe to discuss making a film of a novel of mine that had just been published. He was charming, plausible and enthusiastic; and I was eager that he should stay in such a pleasant frame of mind while we talked about the contract. Unfortunately, however, our cordial negotiations were disrupted by an uninvited visitor. A two-inch cockroach, that pervasive Hong Kong insect, ran up my trousers, prompting an appropriate and immediate response.

My wife struggled to preserve the harmonious atmosphere she had created, but my noisy antics awakened our small son in his bedroom, and I asked the cook to tell the amah that Simon was crying. He returned moments later to report that Ah Ying had not yet finished her own meal and flatly refused to see to the baby until she was through.

I was astonished. Her reaction seemed completely out of character. We had employed Ah Ying for almost a decade and, until that moment, she had never been anything but willing and dutiful. She had been visibly sad on our previous departure from Hong Kong in 1962; and we had employed her again in 1965 when, within three hours of our return, she appeared at our hotel, having been somehow informed of our arrival by her own mysterious sources. How could such a loyal employee, almost one of the family, suddenly be so obdurate? I went to see what was the matter, leaving my wife to cope with the bewildered producer.

I found Ah Ying dedicatedly feeding herself. She had been savouring the food for more than an hour—and was apparently settling down for at least another half-hour. In spite of my pleading that our howling child was jeopardizing an important business transaction, she refused to move until she had finished her deliberate approach to the meal.

Meanwhile our dinner party had degenerated into a farce. I don't believe the domestic disorder queered the motion picture deal; the producer's lack of funds ultimately did that. Still, at the time Ah Ying's perfervid stubborness puzzled me. Now, in retrospect, I believe I understand it. She had, of course, willingly interrupted many meals for the children's sake. But interrupting a meal for *our* sake somehow constituted an unacceptable interference with her personal rights. Her outrage at that ultimate violation was not merely Cantonese but common to the natives of all parts of China—otherwise quite divergent—who make up almost all of Hong Kong's population.

Hong Kong is no Paris hallowed by the shades of time and memories of great events. Its history, as I have already indicated, has been short and rarely glorious; its progress is marked not by splendid old buildings, but by the bulldozer's barren spoor. Nonetheless, I am convinced this city excels even Paris in its gastronomic achievement. I have had mediocre and even bad meals in Paris in the normal course of dining out. But it requires a deliberate effort to get a bad—or even mediocre—meal in any one of the thousands of Hong Kong restaurants that service the universal Chinese passion for good food. (I am not, of course, including the Western-style restaurants that cater to non-Chinese belongers, to tourists, and to the young trendies who consider "eating foreign" the last word in sophistication, but later revert gratefully to their native fare.)

Amid a selection of chicken eggs, a poultry-produce stall in an open-air market presents a tempting centrepiece: a basketful of comparatively scarce speckled quail eggs, which are prized by Hong Kong palates.

If the quality of Chinese cooking in Hong Kong is spectacularly high, its variety is even more remarkable. In a rare moment of less than absolute self-confidence, General Charles de Gaulle groaned of France that it was virtually impossible to govern a nation that produced 400 varieties of cheeses. Admittedly, cheese is one of the very few things that the Chinese *don't* normally eat in Hong Kong. Still, I wonder what de Gaulle would have said if he had shared my experience of dining with some frequency at the Mei Li Chien (American) restaurant in the Wanchai district, which specializes in northern cooking from Shantung province. Even before the restaurant became popular and expanded, when it was hardly more than a cubby-hole off the street, I can remember its offering a menu that included three close-printed pages listing 253 different varieties of noodles, dumplings and bread; and that selection was, of course, supplemental to its catalogue of hors d'oeuvres, appetisers, main dishes, soups and desserts.

In Hong Kong, if one's nerves and stomach could sustain the effort, it would literally be possible to dine out every night for two years at a different restaurant without repeating a single dish. No longer, because of inflation, a shopper's paradise, Hong Kong remains a place to eat Chinese food at its finest—one rivalled only by Taipei, the capital of Taiwan. At one time Peking was also a serious contender. But not any longer, as I discovered on my last visit there. In the People's Republic, even Chinese dedication to the service of the taste-buds is now generally limited by Marxist dedication to austerity.

In spite of the astonishing variety available at the American, my wife and I tended during our visits there to adhere to a fairly standard menu. Like all true Hong Kong belongers, we considered ourselves connoisseurs of Chinese food and we had—by delicious, protracted trial—determined for ourselves what dishes the chefs prepared best. Our standard menu would begin with a cold dish: *peng-peng chi*—the Szechwan province speciality that consists of slivers of chicken breasts on noodles, covered with a fiery chilli-and-sesame sauce; or *chi-ssu la-pier* (literally "chicken slivers and piquant noodles")—much the same as *peng-peng chi*, but a northern version that involves mustard and soya sauce; or *Chengtu pai-chieh jou*, another Szechwan speciality—thinly sliced pork (*the* meat to the Chinese) drenched with garlic, chillies, vinegar and soya sauce.

Our favourite hot dishes were: *kung-pao ta hsia* (palace guard big shrimp)—a Szechwan dish, the shrimp fried in batter and served in a garlicky orange-coloured sauce; *ching-tsau pai-ku*—the familiar spare ribs cooked in all regions of China, but fried lightly instead of deep, and *ho-tsai dai-mao* (varied provender wearing a hat)—a typical northern dish of mixed vegetables and meat capped by an omelette and accompanied by a fragrant plum sauce. The diner makes his own individual portions encased in *pao-ping* (thin wrapping bread).

We would normally omit soup at the end of the meal in order to leave room for *mung-mien*—soft brown noodles made from *mung* beans, a northern speciality. And if the children were with us, their final courses, would be obligatory: for my daughter, *bao-tze*—steamed white buns stuffed with meat or sweet bean-paste; for my son, *chiao-tze*—delectable pork dumplings served as *shui chiao* (boiled), *cheng chiao* (steamed), or *kuo-tieh* (fried). Beyond choosing the method of preparation, my son (who may hold the *chiao-tze* eating championship of Hong Kong, junior division) could have ordered his favourite dish in a number of other guises: as vegetarian dumplings, originally devised for devout Buddhists, or dumplings filled with beef, mutton or shrimps instead of pork. And if we felt so inclined, there was always *tsung-yu ping* onion cakes fried in oil to a most satisfactory crunchiness. But I am making my mouth water— and I have described no more than 2 per cent of the resources of one inexpensive, unpretentious restaurant.

As I have said, all Hong Kong Chinese consider themselves gourmets— and it is my confirmed belief that most of them are. Their expertise extends beyond knowledge of the varied cuisines (although they naturally feel that the dishes of their own ancestral regions are the best) and knowing the diverse methods of preparation. Sprung from an agricultural people, they are still intimately familiar with the raw materials upon which the cook's talents operate. One of the worst insults you can offer a Chinese has remained the same for almost three thousand years: *Wu ku pu fen*—"You can't distinguish the five grains". Obviously, anyone who cannot tell wheat, sesame, barley, beans and rice from each other—much less name them—is the worst kind of dunderhead. I have seen a distinguished professor of the Chinese classics at Columbia University flush bright-red with anguished embarrassment when he could not tick off immediately those five staples.

Sharing a communal platter and helping to serve each other, a family dines with gusto at one of the fish restaurants afloat on barges in Aberdeen harbour.

Just as Hong Kong led me towards a suspension of disbelief in Chinese superstitions, so it undoubtedly endowed me with a lasting enthusiasm for Chinese food. Actually my own attitude towards food, like that of the Chinese themselves, transcends enthusiasm. I, too, feel there is something holy about the fruits of the earth provided for men, and I share their almost idolatrous admiration for the culinary artists who transform that produce into dishes fit for the Chinese gods themselves. The Hong Kong Chinese are not indulging in hyperbole when they honour their professional cooks with the title *Ta Shih Fu*—Great Master.

Good chefs are accorded extraordinary adulation in Hong Kong; their movements are followed as anxiously and inquisitively as the lives of the latest entertainment stars. Since the chef makes the restaurant, top cooks are sometimes given star billing, their names appearing in large characters on the fronts of the establishments. Some Hong Kong chefs operate as self-employed consultants, receiving sizable fees from several restaurants at once. In exchange, a consultant trains the restaurant's kitchen staff and occasionally comes in to supervise personally the cooking for large or important parties of diners.

Restaurateurs constantly try to lure prized cooks from each other with offers of higher salaries or shares in ownership. When such an inducement succeeds, news of the coup—which can mean financial success for the victorious proprietor and possible ruin for the loser—spreads rapidly, since chefs and restaurants are a prevalent theme of daily conversation. Just about everyone exchanges tips on newly promising restaurants and warnings about declining ones. Foreigners, too, can play this ceaseless, keenly contested game; but rarely—if ever—do they earn the supreme accolade by discovering a good new restaurant before their Chinese friends. Should they do so, the admiration tendered them equals—at the very least—the respect they may command by intimate knowledge of Chinese politics or literature.

Of the cuisines available in Hong Kong, that of Peking and northern China —now gaining popularity in Europe and America—is at once the most elaborate and the most primitive. An incredibly wide-ranging category, it can arbitrarily include Muslim dishes—based on mutton and beef, rather than pork—as well as the pungent delicacies of Honan province, such as sweet-and-sour Yellow River carp, or the hearty, barbecued meats favoured in Manchuria. However, for practical purposes, the food of Peking— sometimes rich in rice wine stock, may be taken as a standard.

No Peking speciality is more familiar than that known in the West as Peking duck. Sometimes called "duck-six-ways" by the Chinese, it is more a complete meal than a single dish. Because food has often been scarce in China, the people have learned to consume almost anything that is edible and have made an art of necessity by preparing diverse materials with

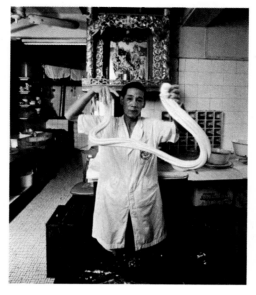

Conjuring up Noodles

The art of drawing out noodles by hand demands the timing and dexterity of a snake wrestler. Here, in the kitchen of a Hong Kong restaurant, a master chef demonstrates with dizzy speed his technique, perfected over a period of 25 years—including a 10-year apprenticeship in Shanghai. After spending a few minutes pounding the noodle paste in order to reduce it to the proper consistency, he twirls a cable of dough in the air for about 40 seconds, doubles it, stretches it, and redoubles it until it divides into ribbons. With each folding the ribbons get thinner and thinner and multiply in number until the chef has an impressive curtain of noodles that are then ready to be boiled or fried.

exceeding skill. Peking duck is a sophisticated example of Chinese frugality; they use everything—as people are fond of saying—but the quack.

The plump birds, having been force-fed like Strasbourg geese, are glazed and roasted. Then the crisp skin is sliced into strips and served with plum sauce, sliced raw cucumbers, spring onions and soft, paper-thin *pao ping* pancakes in which the diner wraps all those ingredients. Often the bloated livers, quick fried, precede the chief dishes; and after the main course comes the remaining duck-meat braised with bean sprouts; that in turn is followed by a custard made with the duck's fat, a soup made of the carcass and a duck-flavoured millet gruel.

Less well-known northern dishes range from chicken velvet—a creamy purée of pulped chicken that turns to floating fragments of delectable fluff when cooked in a soup—to a sturdy mixture of fried pig's liver and tree fungi, served in a wine sauce. One of my own favourites is *shuan yang-jou* —slices of mutton cut so thin that they are cooked in a matter of seconds when the diner himself dips them into boiling stock held in a brass vessel called a *huo-kuo* (fire-pot). Served with sesame-seed rolls, *shuan yang-jou* is accompanied by a sauce each diner mixes for himself from ingredients that include vinegar, wine, soya sauce, coriander, pickled cabbage, sugar, Chinese chilli-sauce, fermented bean-curd and sesame paste. The dish was originally Mongolian, like its twin, *kao yang-jou*—mutton slices broiled on a charcoal brazier. Some connoisseurs affect to look down on both these ancestors of Japanese *sukiyaki* as somewhat primitive. But I can remember those same gourmets descending like starving Mongol hordes on a restaurant near the racecourse in Hong Kong's Happy Valley to consume *shuan yang-jou*, known as a cold-weather dish, as soon as the thermometer gave them an excuse by dropping a few degrees.

Perhaps the most refined cuisine in Hong Kong's repertoire is that of the eastern region of China. Some purists contend that it is not so much a distinct cuisine as a hodge-podge of cooking styles and dishes from various coastal provinces that have been elaborated and perfected by the chefs of sophisticated Shanghai, the country's largest metropolis. Eastern, or Shanghai, cooking is characterized by generous yet discriminating use of salt, sugar and soya sauce (Fukien province on the coast makes China's best soya sauce) and dishes thick with sauces. This is not to say that the region's cuisine is heavy or stodgy; it is famous for delicately flavoured meat and fowl dishes, and for fine, clear soups.

However, the coastal cuisine's strongest emphasis—naturally—is on seafood. Happily, in Hong Kong—which is also on the sea—many of Shanghai's best dishes can easily be replicated. Some, however, are possibly too adventurous for Western tastes—for example, "drunken shrimp", which is precisely what the name implies: tiny, live shrimps swimming in a mixture of wine, water and ginger. I have, perhaps cravenly, never tried that delicacy. But I did once order "green shrimp", which I

On patrol in the New Territories, British infantrymen search an eerily deserted hamlet. A local policeman, at right, supplied an unexpected solution to the mystery: all the inhabitants had left to join relatives who had opened Chinese restaurants in London.

myself had never tried, for a visitor from the U.S. Discovering that it was the same as "drunken shrimp" without the wine, I could only plead ignorance. My guest didn't believe me.

But the *pièce de résistance* of eastern cuisine appeals to all. Every autumn, great red signs with enormous black characters blossom on the fronts of Hong Kong's restaurants: FRESH SHANGHAI CRAB. The Cantonese, who dote on their own salt-water crab, lead the rush to consume the "foreign" delicacy, a freshwater creature harvested from the lakes near Shanghai, said to be the purest lakes in China. The dish is expensive; by the time I left Hong Kong the price in dollars ran to double digits for two rather small crustaceans. There is no nonsense about the diner having to crack the claws and shells. The meat and the coral-coloured roe have already been extracted, gently braised in oil and served on a bed of crisp *tou-miao*—pea leaves. There is no easy way to explain the mania for this simple dish, except to say that Shanghai crab is very fat, very delicious and has a certain scarcity value; since it is only available at one time of the year.

An intriguing sub-division of China's eastern cuisine is the style of cooking developed in Hangchow, a coastal holiday resort about 100 miles south of Shanghai that for millennia attracted honeymoon couples. Hangchow also used to be a popular recreation site for tired businessmen who came to revive their weary taste-buds with the town's enticing food and to satisfy other appetites with its skilled courtesans. These men frequently smoked opium in the belief that it improved their stamina for encounters with the ladies. For this reason the cooks of Hangchow developed delicate

Off the shores of the New Territories, log-suspended cages for the breeding of fish create a silvery mosaic around the floating home of a sea-farming family.

dishes especially for the jaded palates of opium smokers, creating tastes that are at once stimulating and soothing.

Regrettably, with the passage of time many Hangchow dishes are becoming more and more elusive in Hong Kong. But of the cuisine's subtle fare that is available I have particularly enjoyed "Beggar's Chicken"—a fowl stuffed with three kinds of herbs and wrapped in lotus leaves prior to baking. In the old days, it was baked in a coating of mud made from the sediment of old rice wine jars, but not enough wine-jar sediment is available now. The dish has become a fixture of eastern cuisine as a whole.

Of all the regional cuisines available in the Colony, that of western China is hardest to find. Few restaurants specialize in this category, which centres on the chilli-hot dishes of Szechwan in west-central China. But it also includes the equally hot but more subtle food of Hunan, a province to the south-east of Szechwan, as well as the pepper-strewn specialities of Yunnan, a mountainous province to Szechwan's south-west. Some Hong Kong restaurants that feature Shanghai fare make an effort to offer at least a few of the better-known dishes from this vigorous cuisine, such as: sour-hot soup, spiced deer tendon and—as an appetiser—shreds of highly spiced bean-curd skin. And I could never resist Szechwan duck.

The Szechwanese prepare duck in two highly idiosyncratic ways. My favourite is *chang-cha ya*—camphor-tea duck, smoked over a fire of camphor-wood and tea leaves. At its best it is distinctly superior to the smoked goose of Alsace. The other style—equally characteristic but, to my taste, slightly less attractive—is the dish familiarly known in the West as "Szechwan duck", termed by the Chinese *hsiang-su ya* (fragrant-crisp duck). Flattened and steamed in advance, and then fried just before its presentation, it is served with steamed rolls and a roasted mixture of salt and Szechwan pepper, which has a distinct flavour and is hot enough to numb the mouth. Sadly, however, a tomato paste has been insinuating itself on to the platter in recent years, even though the tomato (known as "Western pomegranate") is one of the very few edibles most Chinese do not really relish.

A few other Szechwan dishes to follow those star turns are: *ma-po tou-fu* (pock-marked old lady bean-curd), a ubiquitous, protein-rich cake of pressed ground soya beans sauced with ground meat and chillies to make a kind of hot Chinese spaghetti Bolognese; *tou-ban yü* (speckled bean fish), with the unique sauce, at once subtle and hot, that flavours so many Szechwan dishes; and *yü-hsiang jou-sze* (fish-flavoured meat slivers), a cunningly contrived concoction that gives pork the subtle flavour of sea-fish, which are unobtainable in the inland province of Szechwan.

Fish and other seafoods are, of course, easy to obtain in Canton on China's south coast and they are a prominent feature in southern, or Cantonese, cooking—the "home cooking" of Hong Kong, whose population is basically Cantonese. Because so many of the 19th-Century

Terraced rice paddies hug the hilly terrain in an agricultural district of the New Territories. Such farms make only a tiny contribution to Hong Kong's demand for rice; most of the grain is imported from China, Australia, and South-East Asian countries.

Chinese immigrants to Western countries were from the Canton region, this cuisine also includes a lot of dishes that Americans and Europeans think they know: egg foo yung, egg rolls, beef in oyster sauce, shark's fin soup. I am pleased to say that Hong Kong cooks produce these in so much higher quality than do the majority of those in overseas restaurants that Western visitors to the Colony can look forward to the results as an entirely new taste experience.

Cantonese chefs are experts in stir-frying and they also steam a great many dishes, so southern food is the least greasy of the major cuisines. Many gourmets believe that the southern cooking is China's—and Hong Kong's—most delicious category, but that may be simply because it encompasses such a fantastic variety of subordinate styles, such as the cooking of the Chiu-chow people from Swatow on the coast of Kwantung province, some 200 miles north-east of Hong Kong.

Some of the best seafood I have ever tasted was served at a Chiu-chow restaurant in Causeway Bay. Nothing could surpass the steamed and shelled giant crab claws presented in a light ginger-and-leek sauce. Mind you, it was alarmingly expensive. Whenever I visited this restaurant with foreign friends, the head waiter would ask, in *sotto voce* Chinese, who was paying. If I was paying, he would not suggest crab claws to my guests. At a dollar a claw, it worked out to roughly 50 cents a bite!

Giant conch, minced and braised, is another Chiu-chow dish to delight the palate and deflate the pocketbook. Almost as expensive, ounce for ounce, as Beluga caviar, it is unavailable most of the year in Hong Kong— and perhaps fortunately so. I would make do instead with sautéed fresh scallops on a bed of crisp-fried seaweed, although in these decadent times I would on occasion find that lettuce had taken the place of the traditional seaweed. Tiny, boiled, embryo ears of corn called "jade sprouts" are another speciality. And not to be missed is the delectable swallows' nest soup—the famous broth that many regions of China relish, but which is characteristically Chiu-chow.

Esoteric standards that I do not pretend to understand determine the grading of swallows' nests. It is, of course, well known that the delicious taste is not imparted by the fibrous nest itself but by the glutinous saliva that the swallows excrete to hold the fibres together. But how do you judge the best value for money when shopping for nests? I always wondered about this when I visited the Chiu-chow restaurant at Causeway Bay and looked in its 20-foot-long glass case. Here was a range of swallows' nests available for consumption on the premises or to take home for your own pot. Prices ranged from a modest three or four dollars to $50 or $75. The cost obviously depended partly on size. But the experts, which means most Chinese, could tell immediately from colour and consistency the true worth of those delicacies that look like crudely woven straw baskets. Those experts could also understand far better than I the virtues that make

A kitchen assistant is engulfed in a cloud of fragrant vapour rising from a basket full of steamed dumplings. Filled with chopped meat, seafood or vegetables, the dumplings are usually eaten as snacks or light meals.

the astringent *Tieh Kuan-yin* (Iron Goddess of Mercy)—tea served in thimble-sized cups to begin and conclude the Chiu-chow meal—worth 10 to 20 times more than ordinary tea.

Which Chinese regional cooking is prepared best in Hong Kong? That question is open to endless debate and it will never be resolved. Cantonese cooking naturally dominates Hong Kong. Up to a dozen Cantonese restaurants may adorn a single city block; Cantonese hawkers trundle portable kitchens; innumerable food-stalls line every second side-street; cavernous halls provide lunch-time *dim-sum*—Cantonese pastries and delicacies offered by girls with large trays suspended from straps around their necks. As if that were not enough, every night in the light of acetylene lanterns the entire acreage of the parking lot in front of the Macao Ferry Piers becomes the *Ta Pai Tang* (literally, "Big Signboard Stalls"), with at least a hundred stands bearing signs that proclaim the different Cantonese specialities they offer. Sideshows are provided by jugglers, fortune-tellers and musicians; the Chinese call it the Poor Man's Nightclub (*pages 152-3*).

For richer Cantonese fare I used to visit one of the four Jade Garden restaurants, a chain offering highly innovative food as well as classical Chinese dishes. One of their simplest dishes always delighted me: steamed bean-curd stuffed with shrimps in a light wine sauce. It is ambrosia.

But I was not so delighted when Chinese friends invited me there for a formal party and I was served with a stew enigmatically described on the English-language menu as "snack soup". It was pleasant enough, the unidentified meat tasting like chicken with a rougher texture and more vigorous flavour. But then my pleasure turned to distaste as I discovered from the Chinese menu that the "snack soup" was actually snake soup. My friends were amused by my repugnance. They had anticipated it and yet they could not quite understand it—just as I cannot understand why they won't eat cheese and yet will happily devour fermented bean-curd, which tastes to me like a very ripe Camembert.

Following a 2 a.m. visit to the snake market—an experience that for weeks afterwards imprinted my dreams with writhing forms—I had decided long ago that I wanted no closer contact with reptiles, either swarming in cages or dismembered in a soup bowl. Thankfully, snakes are no longer in such natural abundance in Hong Kong as they once were, but every autumn, when the reptiles are fat enough to satisfy Cantonese gourmets, the creatures are delivered in great quantities from China: rat snakes, cat snakes, cobras and banded kraits, all writhing about in cages and baskets, all ready for the pot.

The Cantonese are perhaps the most catholic of all Chinese in their taste for food that may appear bizarre or distasteful to foreigners. *Heung-yok* ("fragrant meat"—the euphemism for dog's flesh) is still consumed in large quantities in spite of the legal prohibition imposed by the British—a prohibition the locals can no more comprehend than Londoners would understand a regime that banned drinking beer. Similarly, scaly ant-eaters, civet cats, toads and tortoises are all meat to Cantonese cooks.

Such a predilection for strange flesh may have less to do with appetite than a conviction that somehow it is good for you. Hong Kong snake eaters insist that snake meat provides bodily resistance to the cold in winter and that the snake's gall bladder is the supreme remedy for the aches and pains of rheumatism or lumbago. Food and medicine shade into each other here, and the most enthusiastic consumers of the old pharmacopoeia are the Cantonese, who are moved by a veritable compulsion to include medicinals in everyday cooking.

This doesn't mean that you will automatically find the more esoteric offerings in your soup when dining out in Hong Kong—fortunately, because they range from lotus seeds to deer antlers, from dog's testicles to tiger's whiskers, from bat's excrement to fingernail-parings. As for snake meat or young chow dog, no Cantonese restaurant that attracted an appreciable number of tourists would be foolish enough to serve either.

A portion of fried rice in lotus leaf—a Chinese snack available only in summer—is carefully divested of its wrapping to reveal the contents of rice mixed with chopped onions and egg. The leaf is not eaten but has a fragrant smell that blends with the other aromas of the dish.

Nevertheless, sophisticated Chinese from other regions complain that many Cantonese soups are more like a treatment than a treat. In Cantonese restaurants you can obtain chicken broth with *dong-gway*, a root related to mandrake; it is prescribed for pregnant women and for female complaints in general. Equally obtainable—as the prescription for restoring sexual vigour in males—is the same broth infused with ginseng. Altogether, some 2,000 herbs and other substances are guaranteed by their purveyors to restore or enhance virility, make barren women fecund, rejuvenate the nerves, clear the skin, keep one cool in summer or warm in winter—and cure every known ailment. Western doctors in Hong Kong hesitate to decry the Chinese pharmacopoeia as their predecessors did. They have learned that many of the substances are indeed therapeutic.

On the other hand, many middle-aged Chinese inhabitants of Hong Kong feel no hesitation in condemning Western medicine and food. One Cantonese wife expressed herself most succinctly on this subject. I once met her shopping for medicinal herbs to make a soup for her husband. His ailments, as I already knew, included high blood-pressure, a bile-duct obstruction and suspected gallstones. But his doting wife was certain that there was a much simpler reason for his debility. "Western medicines are very bad," she declared forthrightly. "My husband has taken too many foreign medicines. That's why he's ill. Western drugs make you weak."

The woman was equally certain that her own concoction would cure him, and I watched fascinated as she entered a Chinese medicine store in Wanchai. Inside, I saw the wizened proprietor emerge from the back-room into an atmosphere redolent of a hundred different aromas: musk and coriander, rotten eggs and liquorice, ginger, incense and seaweed. From six-foot-high cabinets with hundreds of tiny labelled drawers, he extracted the substances he would compound into a specific for all the ills of his customer's husband. Then, amid the shadows of the macabre shapes hanging from the rafters, he bent over his stone mortar and pestle. The ingredients, I discovered after investigation, were otter's penis, weasel's liver, bear's gall, leopard's bone and rhinoceros horn.

Later I spoke disparagingly about this preparation to a modern-minded, normally sceptical Chinese friend. His aggressive reaction surprised me. "You Westerners depend on penicillin," he flared, "and what's that but mouldy cheese? What makes mouldy cheese a better cure for sore throats than cicada skins? And you eat some strange things: calves' glands, snails and blood-pudding. Chinese medicine and Chinese food have kept us going for many thousands of years—going very well."

And so—I had perforce to agree—they have.

The Liveliest Show in Town

Steered through a market of Victoria by his determined mother—who carries another child on her back—a small boy gazes in happy surprise at a live goose.

Hong Kong's hectic open-air food markets, with their almost ceaseless swirl of buying and selling, are a highly visible—and fragrant—manifestation of the city's devotion to both good eating and profitable trade. There are some 40 of these street markets, and every day they are charged with the enticing aromas of exotic foods and the heady vibrancy of commerce. Mothers shopping for family meals jostle with buyers from small restaurants. Probing fingers test the plumpness of live fowl and the freshness of vegetables. Competing with the stall owners for the custom of Hong Kong's buyers are some 42,000 pedlars (a quarter of them unlicensed) who mill about the streets hawking the produce they carry in baskets slung from their shoulders. Business stays brisk throughout the day, and some of the markets keep trading late into the night.

A vendor of wind-dried sausages weighs an order on a hand-held balance.

A stallholder adjusts her scales to accommodate bundles of white cabbage.

A hawker rearranges the bananas in one of her baskets. When she is walking, the heavy baskets hang from the ends of a pole balanced across her shoulders.

Like many Hong Kong mothers, this woman carries her baby in a back sling as she shops in the market.

A boy almost too big for a sling looks around as his mother buys oranges.

Lulled by movement, a child dozes as his mother purchases pomegranates.

A shopper probes for the best specimens of fish she needs for the day's meal. Local waters provide about a dozen species to delight Hong Kong gourmets.

On the site of a daytime car park, this market, known as the Poor Man's Night Club, sparkles into life each evening, offering cooked food from open stalls.

6

Window into China

From the beginning, China has been Hong Kong's *raison d'être*. Since 1949, when the Communists seized power and erected a wall of secrecy around their new People's Republic, this has become an even greater truism. The Colony has continued to depend on the China trade for essential supplies. In the meantime, Hong Kong has increasingly assumed a role in gathering information about China. Today, in fact, the diminutive territory serves the outside world as an unrivalled window on a nation of more than 800 million people, representing a quarter of mankind.

Because of its modern role as a listening-post, Hong Kong has often been compared to the Lisbon of the Second World War. This, however, is a misleading comparison. The assembly of hundreds of the China Watchers of many nationalities—along with scores of Communist functionaries who busy themselves watching Hong Kong and the China Watchers—has produced a concentration of intelligence activities even greater than Lisbon knew during the war. Moreover, unlike the melodramatic world of espionage associated with the wartime Portuguese capital, Hong Kong's intelligence operations are more overt than covert.

For example, everyone knows that the closely guarded, antennae-crowned offices of the New China News Agency, on Sharp Street in Causeway Bay, have two additional functions—as the unofficial embassy of the People's Republic, and as an outpost for Peking agents who are occupied with countering the activities of Chinese Nationalist agents almost as much as they are with carrying out routine intelligence. These offices may also be the headquarters of the Chinese Communist Party in Hong Kong. Similarly, it is common knowledge that the American Consulate-General in Garden Road, also sprouting its own antennae, is the plexus of Washington's information-gathering. Not without reason is this the largest U.S. Consulate-General in the world.

Some years ago the American government decided that it was advertising its massive presence unnecessarily by listing more than 70 consuls, vice-consuls and attachés in the Hong Kong telephone directory. Subsequently, the new edition of the telephone book listed only a single number for the Consulate-General and another for the residence of the Consul-General. Yet the third floor of the building continued to advertise the special quarters of the Central Intelligence Agency; it was the only section where the silver tapes of burglar alarms were visible on windows shielded by both venetian blinds and curtains. The British Joint Intelligence Committee was less obvious, as were the agents of a score of other nations.

At Lowu railway station on the border between China and the New Territories, two soldiers of the People's Liberation Army keep watch on all activities on the Hong Kong side. In front of them walks a woman whom they recognize and allow to pass over to Hong Kong unhindered.

Nevertheless, the profusion of such agents, overt and covert, was so great that one Hong Kong newspaper editor observed: "It's impossible not to be aware of foreign agents in the Colony. You practically stumble over them at every official reception."

Espionage and information-gathering have long since become a thriving business in this inherently commercial city, virtually an industry in itself. Information is worth money because China so assiduously seeks to prevent the outside world's knowing the details of its internal life. Consequently, many self-appointed freelance agents peddle their wares on the open market. More often than not, as I frequently discovered for myself when offered "inside" stories about developments in China, some of the information is likely to be pure invention. No matter. The great game goes on as energetically as ever; just one more example of Hong Kong's compliance with the laws of supply and demand.

Propaganda, of course, plays an important part in sustaining the underground ideological war being fought on Hong Kong soil, and its principal battlefield is the Colony's bewildering assortment of publications: more than 80 newspapers and at least twice as many magazines. Many are politically biased, and it shows: a pro-Peking newspaper reporting one day that American agents had infiltrated more than 400 industrial and commercial concerns in Hong Kong, a pro-Nationalist newspaper retaliating the next day with an analysis of the ever-increasing Communist grip on the Colony's trade unions.

The neo-Byzantine intrigue in this city is extraordinary by any standards. What makes it even more remarkable is the fact that so much political activity rages in a territory that, officially, has no politics of its own. Hong Kong may be a bastion of free enterprise and a refuge for millions of people seeking to preserve their individual freedom, but let no one be misled. It is not, and has never claimed to be, a territory run on democratic principles. To be sure, half of the 24-member Urban Council is elected by the taxpayers, property-owners, civil servants and professional men and women who qualify for the vote. But this council's responsibilities are restricted to organizing and managing municipal services ranging from public recreation facilities to sanitation and funeral parlours. Actually, all governmental power stems from Britain's monarch—or, more precisely, from the Crown's ministerial advisers. They choose the non-partisan civil servant who heads the Hong Kong government as Governor and Commander-in-Chief. The Governor, in turn, presides over the Executive Council and Legislative Council (both of which are appointed by the monarch, or by the Governor on the instructions of Britain's Secretary of State for Foreign and Commonwealth Affairs), and he has power of assent over all Bills passed by the Legislative Council before they become law.

Since there has been no mass public demand for a fundamental change in the Colony's constitution, one might conclude that the majority of

Signs advertising the services of dentists and herbal healers jut in confusion above a street in the Walled City of Kowloon, a six-acre enclave exempted from a treaty signed in 1898 and still possessed by China. Because law enforcement is minimal there, the district has become a centre for shady dealings and marginal professionals: even dentists can set up practice without bothering to apply for a licence.

residents favour the status quo. More accurately, this acceptance signifies widespread recognition of the fact that there is no practical alternative to colonial rule. Everyone knows that any significant move towards a system of self-government would signal the immediate intervention of Peking, which holds Hong Kong to be strictly a part of the People's Republic—territory "on loan" to Britain for as long as it suits China's own purposes. Obviously, Peking could never tolerate the existence of an independent Chinese government on Chinese soil.

Of course, as some democratic-minded clubs and associations in Hong Kong are quick to complain, many residents are guilty of unreasonable political apathy. Less than a tenth of the qualified electorate bothers to register for the vote in Urban Council elections, and only about a quarter of these actually cast their ballots. But this is apathy on the domestic level where, to be realistic, no significant political advantage is to be gained. The real politics of Hong Kong are on an international scale and, directly or indirectly, they are the concern of all four-and-a-half million of its people.

Every October brings to Hong Kong a forceful reminder of Aristotle's dictum that man is by nature a political animal. On the first day of that month Communist flags and posters celebrate the day (October 1, 1949) when Mao Tse-tung stood at Tien An Men, the Gate of Heavenly Peace, and proclaimed the establishment of the People's Republic. Nine days later, on the so-called Double Tenth, the opposite side of Chinese political life manifests itself. Nationalist flags and slogans bedeck the city in celebration of the revolution that exploded on October 10, 1911, leading to the overthrow of China's Manchu government and the establishment of the Chinese Republic with Dr. Sun Yat-sen as its first president. Ironically, during my last years in the Colony, the Nationalist flags seemed to outnumber the red flags, especially in the working-class districts—largely as a gesture against the Communists' often harsh rule of the Motherland.

How many of Hong Kong's people are actually Communists, Nationalists, Democratic Socialists or whatever? Without an election dipstick, it is impossible to say. Obviously, because so many fled China after the 1949 revolution, the majority are non-Communist, although not necessarily Nationalist. At the same time, the Chinese Communists are a very real force in Hong Kong. They own roughly a thousand enterprises, including 13 local banks, some 50 department stores, several insurance companies and financial syndicates, an assortment of restaurants, shops, petrol stations and publishing companies. More importantly, they command a majority of the trade unions (the pro-Taiwan block of unions is far less well organized); and, of course, they own the Bank of China, which collects an estimated 40 per cent of the People's Republic's foreign exchange.

In terms of political intrigue, the Nationalists have often given Hong Kong's security police more problems than their Communist counter-

A covered railway bridge (right) over the Shum Chun River, at Lowu on the northern border of the New Territories, connects Hong Kong to China. But only freight may actually cross by rail. Passenger trains stop at the bridge, and everyone must alight, walk across, and board another train to continue their journey.

The village of Sha Tau Kok (above) manages to straddle the Hong Kong-China border. The large stone at rear—below the balcony where a Communist guard is peering through binoculars —marks the boundary. Known villagers may cross the border at will, but strangers in the small community are singled out and stopped.

parts. The 1967 riots were a notorious exception, almost certainly having been staged by the local Communists to impress the Peking regime. For the greater part, the Peking line has been that, since Hong Kong exists to serve the People's Republic, it should therefore be allowed to operate efficiently without disturbance. So Communist agents tend to avoid provocative action. In contrast, Nationalist caches of firearms and ammunition are often uncovered by police raids—usually following anonymous tips believed to have emanated from Communist agents. And, over the years, a great many alleged subversives (I say "alleged" because they were never brought to trial) have been deported to Taiwan.

The number of Communist agents deported has been comparatively small, at least as far as the record shows. But then one never really knows. The spy game being what it is, in Hong Kong one can never be sure of a person's political loyalties. I can best illustrate this point by recounting what I know about one of the most infamous cases of cloak-and-dagger skulduggery in the Colony's history: the mystery of the *Kashmir Princess*.

The story began in April, 1955, when an Air India Constellation, the *Kashmir Princess*, exploded shortly after take-off from Kai Tak Airport. The plane was carrying Chinese Communist delegates and journalists en route to the Afro-Asian Conference at Bandung in Indonesia, and 16 lives were lost when it plunged into the South China Sea. The Red Chinese Foreign Ministry insisted that the plane had been sabotaged; furthermore, the Ministry said that it had forewarned the Hong Kong authorities of a plot to destroy an Indian aircraft on charter to Peking. The motive? Chou En-lai himself had been scheduled to make the flight.

Fortunately for China and the world, Chou En-lai postponed his own trip and lived on for an additional 21 years as China's pre-eminent diplomat. Nevertheless, the implications for Hong Kong were positively alarming—especially after a Commission of Inquiry had established "beyond reasonable doubt" that the airliner had indeed been sabotaged, probably by a bomb planted in a wheel-well. It meant that Hong Kong's relations with China were at risk, as was the reputation of the Hong Kong police who had mounted guard on the plane at Kai Tak.

The Hong Kong government immediately promised the most thorough investigation and the Commissioner of Police offered a $17,000 reward—the highest in the Colony's history. One month later the police had identified their prime suspect: Chow Tse-ming, an airfield employee who had helped clean out the sabotaged aircraft during its Hong Kong stop-over. They set out to arrest Chow, but it was too late. Just a few hours earlier, the alleged assassin had fled to Taiwan, reportedly by stowing away on an aircraft of Civil Air Transport, the Chinese Nationalist airline.

The Hong Kong authorities then sought to have Chow extradited to face a charge of conspiracy to murder—in vain, of course. Nonetheless, the fact remained that the Hong Kong police had done a fine, objective

A stall at the Lok Ma Chau post on the China-Hong Kong border offers souvenirs for the tourists who come to gaze across towards China. Alongside the display of silk dolls, plastic chopsticks and paintings are English, German and Chinese versions of Chairman Mao's Little Red Book of Selected Quotations.

job of investigation. Or so we all thought. In particular, I was impressed by John Tsang, an urbane police inspector, who spoke English and Mandarin as fluently as his native Cantonese, and who combined great intelligence and personality. In spite of failure to arrest the saboteur of the *Kashmir Princess*, no one was surprised a few years later when Tsang was promoted to Assistant Superintendent and made Deputy Commandant of the Police Training School. Indeed, he was expected to advance still further.

John Tsang did—but not in the expected direction. In October, 1960, he was arrested as a Chinese Communist spy. He had come under suspicion on his return from a year's professional study in England. Acting on a tip-off, the Hong Kong police had intercepted parcels containing wads of Hong Kong dollar bills. Those notes—duly marked and then allowed to go on their way—led them directly to Tsang. The authorities concluded that Tsang had been steadily supplying Communist China with information about Hong Kong's security plans and the activities of civic leaders. He was deported to Canton.

Security has cloaked many details of this intensely embarrassing affair. But some years later I learned something more surprising about John Tsang. A senior government official confided to me that the disgraced police chief had helped the saboteur of the *Kashmir Princess* to escape, warning him of his impending arrest and assisting his flight to Taiwan.

It was several years before I myself came to appreciate fully the extent of political intrigue in Hong Kong. I suppose that the biggest eye-opener came through my regular contact in the 1950s with Civil Air Transport. The airline had been organized shortly after the Second World War by Major-General Claire Lee Chennault, wartime commander of the U.S. air forces in China. In those palmy days, CAT played a big part in our lives because correspondents (and clergymen) were provided with permanent passes to take free flights whenever they wished.

Eventually, however, my reporting duties brought me into conflict with CAT. I ran foul of the airline by probing too curiously into an incipient scandal over misappropriation of their funds by a trusted accountant. By Hong Kong's standards the story was very small potatoes indeed. Yet I was invited to a sumptuous penthouse on Victoria Peak to be plied with gin—and threats. A senior CAT official, who has since died, warned me that I would suffer unspeakably dire consequences if I persisted in my investigation. Those consequences were never quite spelt out, but I was made aware that they would be much worse than suspension of my free-flight privileges. There was cold menace in the air—as if I were facing not respectable businessmen, but a kangaroo court.

CAT, as I learned soon afterwards, had more to hide than the peccadilloes of an accountant. Through a deliberately bewildering network of interlinked corporations, it served the U.S. Central Intelligence Agency in

ASSOCIATED PRESS

Refugees storm a barbed wire barrier erected by the Hong Kong authorities in May, 1962, when the Chinese Communists threw open their border with the Colony as a means of easing internal unrest at the time. In that one month more than 50,000 Chinese gained asylum in already crowded Hong Kong, but by the end of May others were being turned back by the busload; some, such as the man in the photo on the right, did not give up easily.

the Far East. In 1954, when the American CAT pilot Allan Lawrence Pope was shot down and captured while flying a B-26 bomber over Indonesia, it became clear that CAT was providing aircrews to the CIA-supported rebels against the regime of President Sukarno, in addition to flying regular passenger and cargo runs that were perfectly innocent.

In retrospect, it seemed an obvious extension of the airline's original activities. After all, CAT pilots had included veterans of the "Flying Tigers" (the American volunteers who, under Chennault's command, flew shark-toothed P-40 fighters in defence of Chiang Kai-shek's China before the U.S. entered the Second World War in the Pacific). On occasion their post-war flight assignments had little to do with civil aviation. At Gingles, the Kowloon restaurant that was their unofficial club, they sometimes talked openly about their latest exploits in flying beneath the Communists' rudimentary radar-screens to drop American agents far inside China.

Although the CIA's involvement with CAT was not quickly obvious to me, I was always aware of the agency's operations in Hong Kong; they were, and probably still are, astonishingly conspicuous. During my years there I encountered several obvious CIA agents half-heartedly pretending to be businessmen. Deep cover, it seemed, was not considered important. Successive CIA station chiefs came to work at the U.S. Consulate-General as punctually and as publicly as any Foreign Service officer.

On the other hand, members of the Soviet KGB were badly handicapped since they lacked an official establishment to use as a cloak for their espionage activities. The Russians were not allowed a consulate in Hong Kong; and their correspondents were never granted visas. The Soviet riposte was to appeal to Hong Kong's avidity for profits—by sending their ships into the harbour for repairs. Every Soviet vessel carried stewards and deckhands who spoke fluent English and/or Chinese, and I particularly

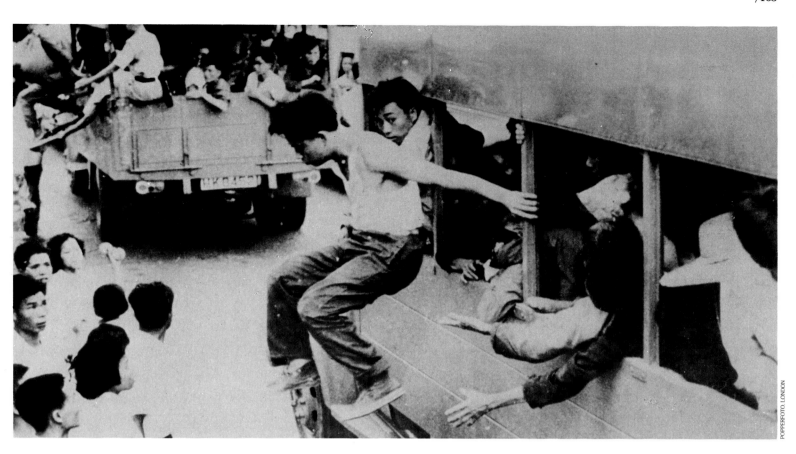

POPPERFOTO, LONDON

remember the liner *Sovetskii Soyuz* putting into the harbour with a "crew" that included eight professional Sinologists from the Faculty of Oriental Studies at Vladivostok's Far Eastern University.

During their port-calls, Soviet crewmen sometimes organized public dances and folk recitals. Other "crewmen" busied themselves recruiting Hong Kong Chinese into spy rings aimed at penetrating the People's Republic. When a major ring was exposed in 1972, the Hong Kong authorities put a Chinese businessman aboard a Russian container-ship for deportation. After four months of haggling, the captain finally sailed, taking the unmasked spy with him.

As far as can be determined, the KGB has not done at all well in Hong Kong; its operations appear to be relatively ineffective. Nonetheless, the Kremlin persists. Like other foreign powers, the Russians have no real choice in the matter. Hong Kong remains the city where men can meet most freely and most usefully to study the mysteries of China. In 1972— one year before the United States was granted a diplomatic mission in Peking—Chou En-lai remarked that Americans in Hong Kong knew more about the People's Republic than did the Russians with all the resources of their vast embassy in the Chinese capital. He was unquestionably right. Even today, when Peking once again has a large diplomatic community and a sizable foreign Press corps, Hong Kong China Watchers have a wider array of sources and perspectives on Chinese affairs than the diplomats and newsmen observing China from within.

In recent years, added weight has been lent to that argument by the action of some British, European and Australian news organizations in maintaining China Watchers in Hong Kong while closing down their Peking special bureaux because they were insufficiently productive. But in reality the activities of Hong Kong and Peking-based China Watchers are complimentary, both having their special advantages which, when combined, provide the best and most comprehensive insight into China's affairs.

When I first settled in Hong Kong the principal off-duty base for China Watchers was the Foreign Correspondents' Club, originally founded in Chungking during the Second World War and subsequently dispossessed to a Hong Kong demi-castle on the lower slopes of Victoria Peak overlooking the harbour. The club wasn't, of course, quite as glamorous as it appeared when William Holden played an American journalist against that setting for the saccharine motion picture "Love is a Many Splendored Thing". Nevertheless, its atmosphere was colourful and dramatic.

In those days the business of China-watching depended very largely upon tales told by newly arrived fugitives from the Communist regime. Often I was interviewing refugees who had been lawyers, doctors, editors and generals only a few years before, and their testimony was by no means wholly unbiased. Among the most fascinating were General Wu Ten-chen —a pre-Communist governor of Kwangtung province, and Morris Abraham Cohen—the legendary "Two-Gun Cohen", an Englishman who had been bodyguard to Dr. Sun Yat-sen, and held the rank of general in the Chinese Nationalist Army. The two old gentlemen would sit with me for hours on the club's terrace, recalling past glories and unrealistically plotting new coups. Cohen even attempted to make himself an emissary between the Nationalists and the Communists, both of whom honoured Dr. Sun. But he had little success. He had become as far removed from great events as was the obsolete old warrior General Wu.

For years the continuing influx of refugees from China provided a chief source of information about the closed world of the People's Republic, although, naturally, we utilized many other varied sources of information. Later, as Peking opened its doors wider (the number of embassies there doubled in the latter half of the 1960s) it seemed that Hong Kong's China-watching role might be steadily diminished. In fact, the reverse happened.

Hong Kong's unmatched importance as a listening-post was kept alive because the activities of Peking-based observers remained severely restricted. The China Watcher in Peking was normally confined to a 15-mile radius from the city's centre, and within that radius his scope for reporting the news was strictly limited. He was almost entirely dependent on official government and party pronouncements. His contacts were still tightly controlled so that he talked with very few Chinese, either officials or private citizens. He needed to exercise political discretion in his dispatches, and he had neither the time nor the team of helpers needed to maintain a constant monitoring of Chinese broadcasts.

In contrast, out of necessity Hong Kong's China-watch became more and more systematized. Besides refugees, the observers increasingly employed other sources: Radio Peking and provincial Chinese broadcasting stations; newspapers and magazines, including underground

Only a two-mile swim from mainland China, the tiny island of Ap Chau in the New Territories is a tempting destination for refugees, although the turbulent, shark-infested waters can take a high toll among the would-be escapees. Hong Kong police estimate that freedom breaks to the northern shores of the Colony total about 3,000 a year.

publications smuggled out from the mainland; letters sent to Hong Kong residents from relations in China. At the same time, Western intelligence services had access to photographs taken by high flying reconnaissance planes financed by the CIA and flown by the Chinese Nationalists, as well as other pictures taken by pilotless planes and satellite cameras. Unlike the man in Peking, the Hong Kong observer could operate with total freedom of commentary, and could profit from contacts who were able to speak out candidly, often after demanding anonymity for the sake of relatives left behind in China. He also enjoyed far greater co-operation from diplomats, who did not fear offending the host government.

Looking back to my early days in the Colony, I cannot help feeling that Hong Kong China-watching has become less challenging and exciting in the process of being made a more efficient and scientific art—just as the Correspondents' Club itself has lost a certain glamour in the name of progress, having been moved out of its demi-castle to make way for new high-rises and re-sited in a downtown skyscraper. Significantly, however, the single, most important element in the art of China-watching has remained unchanged over all the years: educated, sensitive intuition, combined with boldness on the part of the reporter. Beyond this, the essential drive-wheels that make the machinery work are the highly intelligent and objective Chinese aides, most of them born on the mainland. A first-class Chinese associate is indispensable to all correspondents and diplomats, even those who, like myself, can speak and read Chinese. No matter how thoroughly the outsider has studied the history and culture of China, his grasp of those complex subjects cannot compare with the instinctive understanding, sustained by great knowledge, that a well-educated Chinese brings to bear on developments in his homeland.

I myself had the good fortune to be guided in Hong Kong by two remarkable Chinese: Liu-Chieh and Yen Kitung. Liu was one of the first refugees I met there. A one-time editor and war correspondent, he possessed immense knowledge of the Chinese military structure and a thorough understanding of the more obscure ramifications of the Communist administration. Yen came to Hong Kong in 1959 after completing his undergraduate studies at Peking's Chinghua University, where he was denied a degree because he became embroiled, on the liberal side, in a major controversy over Chinese literature that had far-reaching political consequences. He had a brilliant mind, and his interpretative genius shone brightest every October 1, China's National Day, when we used to meet in my office to tape and analyse the lengthy broadcast of speeches and commentary from Peking. He quickly took in the meaning of orations spoken in regional accents that differed far more widely than, say, Liverpool English differs from Alabama American; simultaneously he put the salient points into Mandarin that I could understand, and he analysed the true significance behind the Communist leaders' words.

Mobbed by Press photographers, a young Communist addresses a rally of student leftists in Victoria Park. While political parties are not officially recognized by the Hong Kong government, both sympathizers and opponents of Communism can organize public meetings as long as they first obtain a police permit.

The art of China-watching has always depended on such analytical exercises as well as on the tedious reading of every scrap of official information that emanates from the People's Republic of China. During the tumultuous Cultural Revolution of 1966, friends and I ran our own monitoring service because most news of significance came not from embattled Peking but from the broadcasts of provincial radio stations. My wife complained bitterly that she could not walk into any room in our house without finding someone crouched over a tape-recorder. "You've really gone too far this time!" she finally exclaimed. "I just went into the bathroom in my dressing-gown looking forward to a hot bath. And sitting there was a perfect stranger with a radio and tape recorder. Well, at least he didn't object to *my* intrusion."

Characteristically, financial inducements also helped to elicit informative documents. Even more characteristically for Hong Kong, such enterprise generated its own highly specialized form of fraud. One day my almost excessively competent secretary Nancy Lim confided: "I think Mr. Chen is writing letters to himself and putting them into envelopes from China. The last letter he produced was supposed to come from Tientsin. But the postmark was Shanghai, and the handwriting on the envelope was totally different from the letter."

My own favourite fraud was a forged refugee. At a most chaotic moment of the Cultural Revolution, a contact man introduced me to a 42-year-old "professor" who was supposed to have just arrived in Hong Kong from the University of Wuhan, where rival factions of the People's Liberation Army were shooting at each other. Both Nancy and Yen Kitung were dubious about him. So was I when the self-styled professor attempted to speak Mandarin with a heavy Cantonese accent. We politely declined his story.

Soon afterwards I discovered that another correspondent had been only too pleased to get an "exclusive" from the same man. After all, it wasn't every day—or even every year—that a correspondent could talk at length with a refugee who knew all about Chinese nuclear installations! The man's sponsors had forged him a new identity. He was presented as the former official photographer of the Communists' Defence Scientific Research Commission, and the world was duly regaled with an "insider's" extensive view of China's nuclear plants and missile installations, complete to the most minute details—all wholly imaginary.

The moral for reporters seems clear enough: if a need exists, Hong Kong will fill it—one way or another.

City of Extremes

On Causeway Bay, smartly fitted launches lie at spacious Yacht Club moorings across from a tangle of sampans on which entire families live, breed and die.

Although the four-and-a-half million inhabitants of diminutive Hong Kong must, perforce, live in jostling proximity to one another, the economic gulf separating the few very rich from the millions of poor is so broad as to divide the Colony into two different worlds. Rising wages for workers and plentiful opportunities for gifted entrepreneurs are, however, helping to bridge the gap. Still, in a restless society constantly replenished by impoverished immigrants from China, nothing seems more permanent than the polarity of wealth—as even casual glimpses of the Colony will attest. For many Hong Kong residents, the simplest necessities of life—water, a little bit of territory to call home—are difficult to come by; while the very rich live in a splendiferous style that frequently surpasses that of the privileged in any city in the world.

Cocktail party guests at a house on Victoria Peak enjoy blissful freedom from the congestion and steamy heat of the urban reaches hundreds of feet below them.

Down by the waterfront in the North Point area of Hong Kong Island, shacks in a shanty town huddle together in a mass of detritus.

Guests at an official party held to mark the Queen's birthday wander on to the spacious balcony of the Hong Kong Club, still a bastion of colonial privilege.

Boxes serve as furniture for the alleyway home of a family living the hand-to-mouth existence of many immigrants from China.

A pool around columns of a house on Victoria Peak marks the height of affluence, for water on Hong Kong's rocky islands has always been a rare commodity.

With the family laundry hung out to dry, a child commandeers the washtub for secondary use of the water drawn from a near-by standpipe.

7

The Price of Progress

In Hong Kong
They strike a gong
And fire off a noonday gun
To reprimand each inmate
Who's in late . . .

In the spring of 1968, the playwright and entertainer Noel Coward made a return visit to Hong Kong and, with flashbulbs popping all around, solemnly pulled the lanyard of the ceremonial cannon he had celebrated 38 years earlier in the lyrics of his witty song, *Mad Dogs and Englishmen*. As Coward's words originally suggested, the firing each noon of the Colony's famed gun illustrated the peculiar ways of a dwindling breed of tradition-bound British colonials.

Hong Kong's noonday gun belongs to Jardine, Matheson and Co., the great British *hong* of old. In the late 19th Century a number of cannon owned by the company were fired in salute to the head of the firm upon his return from a trip. The company was severely reprimanded by the Queen's senior naval officer on the China Station because, as he explained, such saluting was reserved exclusively for governors and naval officers of senior flag rank. By way of penance the company was ordered to perform a time-keeping service by firing a cannon once every noon until further notice. No one ever remembered to cancel the order. So, very correctly, Jardine's have been firing the cannon ever since—except for the years of the Japanese occupation, when they suspended the custom involuntarily.

In the mid-1970s, as I was leaving Hong Kong permanently, I checked my wristwatch for the last time by the boom of Jardine's cannon. The ritual heightened my nostalgia. The noonday gun was among the few survivals of the Hong Kong I had known as a freshman "belonger" a quarter of a century before. Of course, many of the old sights and sounds remained—but now with some modifications. Victoria Peak, although radically redeveloped, still afforded a breathtaking view of the harbour, even if most of the busy local craft below were now motor-powered. Nathan Road, on the Kowloon side, was still the liveliest street in town, even if it no longer teemed with rickshaw boys vociferously competing with red London-style buses and multi-coloured taxis. At the harbour end of Nathan Road, the old Peninsula Hotel (where Noel Coward typed his final draft of *Private Lives*) still stood tall and dignified, even if interior modernization had destroyed its quaint Palm Court atmosphere of the Victorian era. But, on reflection, I could think of precious few things beyond Jardine Matheson's cannon that were *exactly* the same.

In a crowded tenement, a grinning mother stands guard over her brood. In spite of the Westernizing influences that have given her Hong Kong-reared children jeans and Superman tee-shirts, she has remained faithful to one long-standing Chinese family tradition—fecundity.

As I have already remarked, the pace of change in Hong Kong is so rapid that the Colony would literally be unrecognizable to someone who had not seen it for, say, 30 years. When I look back over two-and-a-half decades, I am staggered by the scope of change in the service of progress and growth. I remember the substantial detached house we occupied in Stubbs Road on the lower slopes of Victoria Peak where miniature barking deer used to nibble at my wife's vegetable garden. Those graceful creatures have now dwindled to a few dozen survivors in the New Territories and in the small densely wooded areas that remain on the island. The house itself has inevitably given way to a 12-storey block of flats. New developments are always rising somewhere: more hotels and apartments, more office space for Hong Kong's 70 or so banks, some 90 major international companies and roughly 36,000 local enterprises.

Confronted with so much innovation and redevelopment, the outsider may well be inclined to view business-dedicated Hong Kong as no more than an animated balance-sheet, with commercial as well as human assets and debits subtly intermingling. Queen's Road Central has long since become a canyon filled with carbon monoxide; at the same time, new centres of commerce and finance are springing up in more salubrious outlying locations, in Kowloon and the New Territories.

The new runway of Kai Tak Airport, 8,350 feet when originally completed in the early 1960s, has crept an additional 2,780 feet into Kowloon Bay; and amid the frantic traffic activity, fishing in the harbour has become a waste of time. On the other hand, landing in Hong Kong is no longer the perilous adventure it used to be, when planes had to approach with one wing cocked high to avoid a mountainside. Moreover, the airport's strategic position at the hub of South-East Asia's air-traffic network has made it a major earner of revenue for the Colony, as well as an important asset to the British government when it bargains with other countries for landing rights. And the depletion of local fishing resources has, to a certain extent, been redressed: the big new fishing junks, all motorized, can now range as far as the waters off Vietnam.

Hong Kong's catalogue of losses and gains is endless since it is constantly changing. While the delicate barking deer have managed to elude extinction, the mid-20th Century has witnessed the total disappearance of many indigenous animals, including tigers and leopards, the large Indian civet, the crab-eating mongoose, the wild red dog and the South China red fox. On the credit side, although rather belatedly, more than half of Hong Kong's 300 square miles of countryside has been placed under protection orders that seek to conserve wildlife, trees and plants.

Has Hong Kong, then, changed for the better or for the worse? There can be no unqualified answer because the judgment must be subjective. Hong Kong is a state of mind, a conscious creation of the indomitable spirit of man, even more than it is a geographical entity or a historical

Metal birdcages cast elegant, parasol-shaped shadows on a mouldering Hong Kong wall. Birds are popular pets among the older generation of Chinese.

accident. One may carefully weigh the advantages and disadvantages of so-called progress, but any conclusion must finally be clouded by one's instinctive approach to Hong Kong itself.

From a strictly personal viewpoint, I must regretfully conclude that the Colony's losses outweigh the gains. When I arrived in 1951 Hong Kong was not polluted by industrialization and modernization. The city was quieter, the countryside largely unspoiled. Moreover, prices were astonishingly low, and on a salary of a mere $60 a week I could enjoy a graceful style of living that would be quite impossible today on many times that amount. But it is all too easy to wax nostalgically over the "good old days" and to forget amid one's warming memories that some grievous inequities prevailed at the time. I don't need to be reminded that hundreds of thousands of refugees were virtually homeless while I was relaxing in the almost palatial surroundings of the Correspondents' Club, and that my meagre $60 a week was at least 10 times the average worker's wage. In those two most important respects—housing and wages—Hong Kong has undoubtedly changed for the better. It may no longer provide such gracious living for the minority, but it does now allow a decent livelihood for the majority of its people.

The newcomer to Hong Kong is still struck by the blatant contrast in the Colony's property development and by the divide between the haves and the have-nots. Many people are still living in squalor. Indeed, statistics indicate that the problem of squatters actually became somewhat worse in the mid-1970s for various reasons: the recession in industry, the continuing influx of immigrants from China, and the clearing of areas marked for new development. But anyone who knew Hong Kong in the 1950s will recognize the extraordinary improvement that has been brought about by the government's housing programme. True, many government-built homes are much less attractive than Oi Man (Love the People), the $37 million public housing development on 21 acres of Kowloon that provides handsome shelter for 46,000 people. Nevertheless, public housing projects—non-existent when I arrived in Hong Kong—now provide low-rent homes for almost half the entire population.

Similarly, Western visitors to Hong Kong still complain about the working conditions in the Colony—most especially about the cruel exploitation of child labour. And such exploitation truly persists, in spite of laws forbidding the employment in industry of children under 14 and dictating that all women and young people 14 to 17 years of age cannot be required to work more than 40 hours a week. But, here again, the improvement on conditions of the Fifties is extraordinary. Since 1967, well over a hundred items of legislation dealing with safety, health, welfare and training have been passed in an effort to improve employment conditions. Many companies provide their employees with bonuses, luncheon vouchers, dormitory accommodation for single workers, and other benefits. And the government encourages healthy trade-union practices, even though many

On a rooftop playground in the crowded Kwun Tong district, schoolchildren perform their daily exercises beneath a wire-mesh screen designed to keep gym equipment from flying out on to the busy street below. Since 1971, free primary schooling has been available for all Hong Kong children aged between five and 11.

Chinese, by tradition and temperament, have no appetite for organized labour. By Western standards, of course, the working conditions remain unsatisfactory. But it needs to be remembered that by Asian standards they are exceptionally good. Only in Japan, Singapore and perhaps Taiwan do Asian workers enjoy equal or better wages and working conditions.

The most striking advances have been in medical care and education. Hong Kong has been made free of epidemics and quarantinable diseases; and many new hospitals, schools and colleges have been built. Although facilities still fall short of the needs of the population, free medical care and surprisingly rigorous public education are increasingly available. Has enough been done? Perhaps not. Certainly it can be argued that ordinary workers have not shared proportionately in the Colony's post-1955 economic boom. The rise in social welfare spending—especially between 1970 and 1975, when it increased by 600 per cent—is not so impressive when you consider that expenditure in the 1950s and 1960s never did represent more than 2 per cent of the Colony's Budget. Nevertheless, the progress—satisfactory or not—has been very substantial and very real.

If one heeds only the Hong Kong government and its apologists, there is a real danger of being sold too cosy a picture of the Colony—an image of a remarkably free and progressive society marred only by the caprices of nature, the uncertainties of the international market-place, and the vagaries of the People's Republic of China. But its problems really go very much deeper than that. Hong Kong is, after all, one of the most material-istic places on earth. The chronicles of its past are, with occasional excep-tions, notable for neither altruism nor sanctity; the most obtrusive reality of its present is the overcrowding, the hard toil, the nerve-wracking strains and constant pressures that make the life of most Hong Kong belongers an unending test conducted according to the ethos of materialism. That test is, of course, integral to the character of the Colony. And because the materialistic competition is so fierce, one major scar on the face of Hong Kong has not significantly changed in all the years I have known it. I refer to the Colony's widespread, deeply ingrained corruption.

Corruption persists partly by way of tradition (cumshaw—bribery—is not a custom peculiar to Hong Kong; it is endemic throughout Asia) and partly through the fundamental get-rich-quick attitude arising out of the Colony's chronically uncertain future. Another key factor is the strength of Chinese criminal associations, similar to the West's Mafia, which thrive on corrupt officials. These groups are generally referred to as "triads"—after the *San Ho Hui*, or Three Harmonies Association (Triad for short), which was the most powerful of a number of secret societies founded by patriots in China to resist the alien Manchus who overthrew the Ming Dynasty in 1644. During the 19th Century, as disorder and rebellion spread through-out China, the societies became extra-legal governments; their members

Prospective art buyers size up an 18th-Century porcelain bowl—one of a matching pair—prior to an auction at the Mandarin Hotel. Collections of antiques brought into Hong Kong by emigrants from China in the late 1940s fostered a lively trade that has continued to this day in spite of China's subsequent ban on the export of art objects.

were afforded protection from the exactions of bandits, soldiers and tax-collectors. Inevitably, extra-legality evolved into illegality. And when the societies set up shop in Hong Kong, they deteriorated into gangs whose business was based on intimidation by terror and extortion by violence.

Hong Kong's triads have an estimated core membership of close to 80,000 in a population of four-and-a-half million. They are involved in all kinds of criminal activity, from protection rackets to drug-running, and some still preserve the chilling rituals of their predecessors. Once or twice a month, groups of teenage youths meet in Kowloon or Wanchai tenements for initiation. They prick their thumbs, mingle their blood and swear fearsome oaths of loyalty, such as "If I break my sacred word, may I be hacked to death by 10,000 knives!" The youths are than pronounced to be "fighters" of the secret society and they are required to follow their inbred inclination towards violence. The next day, the same youths, with knives drawn, may surround a frightened minibus driver and extort two days' earnings in return for their "protection". Others will seduce or rape young girls who thereafter, feeling themselves "spoiled", see no alternative but to begin a life of prostitution under the protection of the triads.

In a community where the traditional Chinese family, once the firm mortar of society, is disintegrating under the impact of urbanization and industrialization, triad membership not only offers a substitute family but also confers a measure of prestige. Triad members are the kings of the streets. Their reputation for violence inspires enormous fear. I know of an incident in which a young triad "fighter" casually fired a home-made zip gun in a restaurant and wounded a waitress. The proprietor's first concern was to avoid offending the triads. He sent the waitress to an unlicensed doctor, after warning her: "We don't want trouble with the triads, do we?" Severe infection subsequently forced the waitress to resort to a government hospital, but neither she nor the proprietor would identify her assailant.

The police, of course, are aware that this sort of thing is common, but usually cannot act without complainants or witnesses. Then, too, they sometimes may choose not to act because precipitate action can result in even greater social disruptions—because the local constable or his sergeant is enjoying a comfortable supplementary income in return for "protection".

The consciousness of substantial corruption among the police has, quite understandably, cast their work against the triads into some disrepute. The most blatant scandal arising from such venality unfolded in 1973, when $40,000 was found hidden in a car belonging to Chief Superintendent Peter Fitzroy Godber, who was the second-ranking policeman in Kowloon. Suspended during the subsequent investigation, Godber fled the Colony, slipping through surveillance at the airport in such haste that he left behind $50,000 in his local bank account. He could afford the sacrifice. It was rumoured that he had already deposited more than $1 million abroad.

Godber was eventually extradited from England. His and similar trials made it clear that he was only one of a number of high-ranking Hong Kong police officers enriching themselves on sums paid by brothel-keepers, gaming-house owners, pimps and drug-pushers of the Colony's underworld. That revelation came as no great surprise. What did shock Hong Kong was the excessive amount of cumshaw being paid to Godber and his confederates.

As one Chinese businessman complained to me: "I can see that a police constable making less than $250 a month has to live. But I can't see that a chief superintendent making $1,500 a month has to prey on the people of Hong Kong so rapaciously." Unfortunately, that same respectable citizen saw no harm in the small-scale sorts of corruption that are ubiquitous in Hong Kong: businessmen distributing "gifts" to facilitate commercial transactions, motorists offering "contributions" to jump ahead in the queue for a driving test or letting banknotes flutter to the pavement when they are stopped for a traffic offence, restaurants paying regular instalments to traffic wardens to keep their customers free from parking tickets.

The blasé view of the citizenry is not always easy to explain, since certain examples of corruption may in fact work disastrously against the public weal. When I first arrived in Hong Kong, a practising architect informed me: "You must assume that contractors will cheat by mixing at least twice as much sand as they should with the concrete and that they will omit as much as half the required steel reinforcing rods. A payoff to the building inspector ensures that he'll turn a blind eye. I've seen the self-same reinforcing rods inserted into one part of a foundation before the adulterated concrete was poured, removed to another part, then shifted again—and finally carted away to play the same farce elsewhere. That building, when completed, may have been braced by only a fraction of the prescribed reinforcement. But I could do nothing. I was told strongly that it wasn't a good idea to protest."

No wonder that buildings on Hong Kong's precipitous slopes have been known to collapse. Twice during my years in the Colony, entire buildings slithered down the hillsides during typhoons. Hardened natives simply shrugged at the extensive loss of life and property, and said that such hazards were only to be expected.

A curious logic underlies this sort of attitude. In Hong Kong you can buy almost anything from a 13-year-old virgin to a 1,300-year-old T'ang Dynasty statuette; both are certified as genuine and, upon occasion, they may genuinely be genuine. So why shouldn't you be able to buy a building inspector, policeman, tax inspector, or government factotum? That is the traditional view of a majority of the people in the Colony and, as the government has long since discovered, nothing—not even drug-addiction—is harder to break than the combination of centuries of deep-rooted Chinese tradition and the *laisser-faire*, buccaneering tradition of the early British merchant-settlers and their successors.

Gorgeously costumed operas still draw crowds at festival time, although Hong Kong has no permanent theatre for this highly stylized traditional art form.

Walking at dawn near a village in the New Territories, three generations of one family create a deceptive image of continuity in a fast-changing society.

Nevertheless, the government tries. In 1974, for example, it established the Independent Commission Against Corruption—independent, that is, of the police and other departments notoriously vulnerable to bribery. This organization was divided into three groups: an operations (investigatory) arm; a branch responsible for examining the procedures and practices of government departments and public bodies with the aim of eradicating or reducing opportunities for corruption; and a group responsible for rallying public support by mass-media campaigns, lectures, and organized discussions. Controversially, the operations arm, manned by 450 detectives, was given powers to detain without a warrant and extensive powers of search, including the authority to examine private bank accounts and to call upon anyone, even a Crown servant, to explain his wealth or living style.

Within three years the commission had brought more than 500 prosecutions and secured nearly 400 convictions. It also attracted bitter criticism on various grounds: invasion of privacy, its possible inhibiting effect on commercial enterprise, its damage to police morale. Nevertheless, it was an important and very necessary first step towards re-educating the public. The government cannot hope to change the general attitude towards petty corruption until it has convinced the public as a whole that corruption has been effectively outlawed in high places and within the Civil Service in particular. In recent years an increasing number of complaints against officials on the take has indicated that some progress is being made in obtaining public co-operation. There is no suggestion here that the war against graft will end in total victory, but the trend is encouraging.

Thus, in myriad ways, great and small, efforts to improve life in Hong Kong are constantly being made, and they have undeniably altered the circumstances of the residents for the better. Even so, two diametrically opposed views of Hong Kong—as a free-enterprise heaven or as an exploitive, capitalist hell—remain widely held. The truth does not conveniently lie somewhere in between. Both extreme assessments are equally accurate—or inaccurate—depending almost entirely on one's political or sociological viewpoint. The truth—if there is a single truth about Hong Kong—lies on an entirely different plane. It is virtually impossible to comprehend the reality of Hong Kong if one views the Colony as a sociological enormity, an ideological case-lesson, or a baroque pawn in the cold war between East and West. The most enlightening approach, I submit, is to look at Hong Kong through its people—the individuals who have created the city, having often wrought better than they intended or worse than they knew.

As I have previously observed, the Colony's inhabitants have been drawn there by many different motives. They include fugitives from economic and political oppression, fortune-hunters lusting after wealth, romantics spurred by idiosyncratically coloured visions of Asia. Yet the great majority have shared certain characteristics and deprivations. Since they arrived alone or, at best, accompanied only by their immediate relations, they were no longer sustained by a wide-spreading family of several generations and many degrees of relationships. So new Hong Kong residents, Chinese or foreign, were impelled to create their own "families"—groups bonded by proximity and common interests more often than by common blood.

This has had an exceptional effect on community relations within such a confined and overcrowded territory. Here, a "circle of friends" virtually constitutes a communal tribe; and even when friends move to another part of the Colony, one is almost certain to encounter them again sooner or later. Offhand, I can think of half a dozen different areas of Hong Kong where I couldn't walk down the street without being greeted by a succession of old friends and acquaintances. Similarly, when my wife returned from a shopping sortie—whether to Central, Aberdeen, Stanley or Causeway Bay—she would invariably recall that she had been delayed by long encounters with familiar faces. "This isn't a village," she used to say. "It's a collection of hamlets." And she was absolutely right. Hong Kong is a congeries of "clan-villages" in the old Chinese manner.

Once acquired, the sense of belonging to a vast, homogeneous family remains indefinitely—even after one has left the Colony. My wife and I came to appreciate this fully during a visit to New York, where we met some old Chinese friends who had emigrated from Hong Kong to the United States. They had successfully adapted to the American way of life, but they were still clinging fiercely to the ties they had formed half a world away; and when we met, they insisted on entertaining us with a sumptuous Chinese meal. Afterwards they lavished gifts upon us, including for each of our children a $100 bill in a little red *lai see* envelope. I then realized that our own children had, as far as possible, been cast to fill the gap of the children in China from whom our friends had been irrevocably separated more than two decades before. I realized, too, that we had all become one family—a true family, regardless of differences in physiognomy, accent and culture.

It was much the same when we attended Prize Day ceremonies at our daughter's school in Surrey, England. Amid the confusion of parents, one group instinctively came together to form a tight-knit unit: the Hong Kong contingent. Some of the parents had left the Colony many years ago, but they all recognized one another and they communicated as naturally and as intimately as if they had been blood relations.

One Hong Kong parent, Mr. Wong, broadly hinted that some of the old Chinese talent had obviously rubbed off on my Hong Kong-born daughter, who had done well enough to win admission to medical school. His remark was a great compliment to a foreigner, and he was almost certainly right. My children are indubitably part Chinese—by instinct and by choice—after so many years in Hong Kong. Why else should they hoard *wah-muis*, a particularly unattractive preserved sour plum, and insist, whether in New York or London, that the first order of business after arrival must be a

Less than three miles from the heart of Kowloon, the lone runway of Kai Tak Airport stretches into Kowloon Bay. The Hong Kong government solved the problem of providing a landing-site for the hilly Colony by reclaiming land from the bay's shallow waters and creating a promontory now nearly two miles long.

Chinese meal? Why else should both their faces light up at visiting Gerrard Street or Mott Street and seeing all those friendly Cantonese faces that appear remote or even sinister to other Westerners who have never known life in Asia? And why else should they instinctively and pityingly refer to such deprived Westerners as "foreigners"?

This sense of belonging is an aspect of Hong Kong life that is rarely, if ever, remarked upon by the travel writers or the political, economic and social observers who visit the Colony. Naturally, they are drawn to more sensational fare: the wheeler-dealering, the corruption, the sweated labour, and the seamy night-life they label as "The World of Suzy Wong" but which —because so many Japanese tourists flock to it—would be better called "The World of Suzuko Wong". Yet, for the residents, this curious kind of togetherness is also an integral part of the Colony.

I call it "curious" because competitiveness rather than togetherness is the obvious keynote of life in Hong Kong. Yet the concepts are linked: the people are conscious of sharing a trial by the ordeal of 20th-Century materialism. Often forced to work against each other, they work for each other when they can. Each small community, like a village in China, asserts its rights and its inhabitants' rights against the outsiders. Each group that claims common origin in a town or province of China co-operates. Even practitioners of the same trade, professions or craft close ranks for common protection. The framework that supports this diverse society is more complex, more intricately joined and much more flexible than any outsider can appreciate. In enduring such grinding toil and discomfort, the people of Hong Kong live with remarkable exuberance—incidentally giving the lie to the Western cliché about "inscrutable Orientals".

There is, of course, little room for sentiment in the affairs of the city itself. The economy of Hong Kong must, like a jetliner, maintain great momentum—or stall and crash. Granting that this relentless pursuit of wealth may be described either as the idealist's quintessential hell or as the pragmatist's hypothetical heaven, Hong Kong nevertheless *works*. Moreover, Hong Kong's effective capitalism shows to great advantage in spite of its many injustices and deficiencies—in contrast with the disorder, wilful or involuntary, that has dominated its gigantic neighbour and landlord, China, during most of the extended period since the Colony came into existence.

As we have seen, that genesis lay in one of the greatest crimes of the 19th Century: the systematic endeavour to inflict opium addiction upon the world's most populous nation. But Hong Kong's survival—nowadays by the explicit tolerance of the same nation—is one of the great miracles of the 20th Century. The anomalous Colony is a triumph neither for colonialism nor for democracy, but for the tenacious spirit of a people possessing endless ingenuity, infinite adaptability and awesome industry. Those attributes have enabled them to make a true homeland out of the gaudiest, most improbable market-place on earth.

Patterns of Living

In spite of the numbered anonymity of identical buildings, this vast public housing project in Kowloon is cherished by the 80,000 immigrants who call it home.

The continual influx of immigrants from Communist China that has served to increase Hong Kong's population sevenfold since 1945 has also profoundly affected the appearance of the compact metropolis. For want of room in which to expand outwards, Hong Kong has been forced to build upwards to accommodate the newcomers. Skeins of bamboo scaffolding that assist the construction of high-rise residential and office blocks have become one of the Colony's most familiar sights. The new buildings, with constantly repeated details of windows and balconies that are often bedecked with family washing, are more utilitarian than beautiful; but their very uniformity, seen from a distant perspective, renders them visually impressive. These structures graphically suggest the awesome size of the housing and working-space problems they were built to solve.

Lights shining in uncurtained flats give a housing estate in Kowloon's Diamond Hill resettlement area the look of an abstract nocturne.

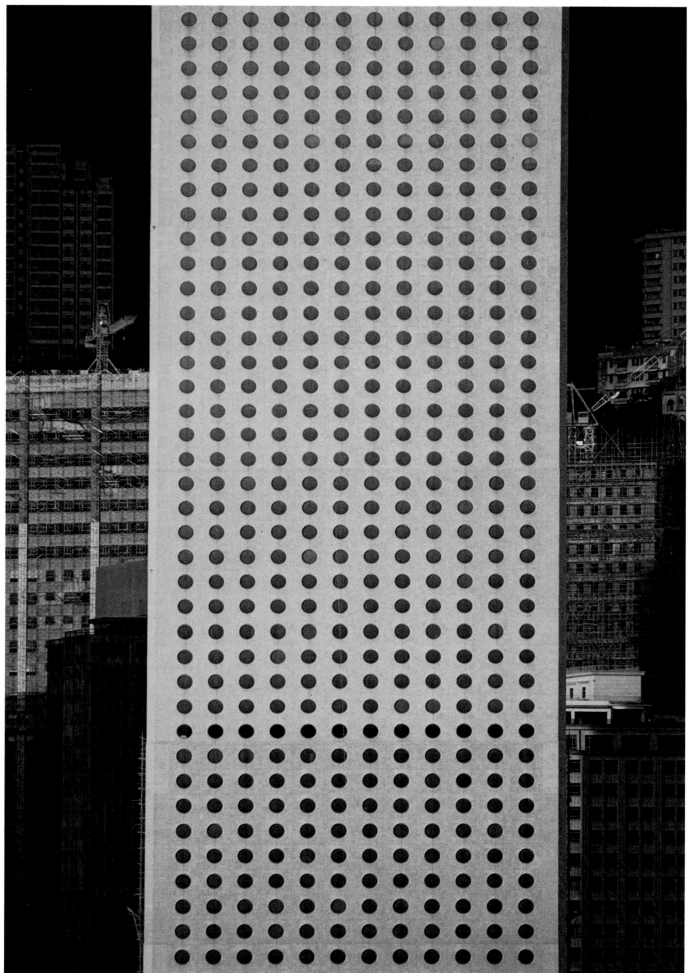

The 52-storey Connaught Centre office tower in Central District became Hong Kong's tallest building when completed in 1973.

Workers on a block of flats are enmeshed in a bamboo scaffolding, cheaper than steel and surprisingly strong in spite of its frail appearance.

Flagstaff-like bamboo poles sprout from the Tsz Wan Shan housing project in New Kowloon as residents hang out their washing.

High-rise blocks of flats in the Mei Foo Sun Chuen housing development cluster above the Kowloon waterfront in an interlocking pattern of concrete and glass.

Bibliography

Burkhardt, V. R., *Chinese Creeds and Customs* (*3 vols.*). South China Morning Post Ltd., Hong Kong, 1954.

Collis, Maurice, *Foreign Mud.* Faber and Faber Limited, London, 1964.

Cooper, John, *Colony in Conflict, The Hong Kong Disturbances May 1967-January 1968.* Swindon Book Company, Hong Kong, 1970.

Eitel, E. J., *Europe in China, The History of Hong Kong.* Luzac & Company, London, 1895.

Elegant, R. S., *The Centre of the World.* Methuen and Co. Ltd., London, 1963.

Elegant, R. S., *Mao's Great Revolution.* Weidenfeld & Nicolson, London, 1971.

Endacott, G. B., *A Biographical Sketchbook of Early Hong Kong.* Eastern Universities Press Limited, Singapore, 1962.

Endacott, G. B., *A History of Hong Kong.* Oxford University Press, London, 1973.

Endacott, G. B., *An Eastern Entrepôt.* Her Majesty's Stationery Office, London, 1964.

Endacott, G. B., *Government and People in Hong Kong 1841-1962.* Hong Kong University Press, Hong Kong, 1964.

Golger, Otto, J., *Squatters and Resettlement.* Otto Harrassowitz, Wiesbaden, 1972.

Hughes, Richard, *Borrowed Place, Borrowed Time, Hong Kong.* André Deutsch, London, 1976.

Ingram, Harold, *Hong Kong.* Her Majesty's Stationery Office, London, 1952.

Jao, Y. C., *Banking and Currency in Hong Kong.* Macmillan, London, 1974.

Jarvie, I. C., ed., *Hong Kong: A Society in Transition.* Routledge & Kegan Paul, London, 1969.

Kirkup, James, *Hong Kong and Macao.* J. M. Dent & Sons Ltd., London, 1969.

Ommanney, F. D., *Fragrant Harbour.* Hutchinson, London, 1962.

Osgood, Cornelius, *A Study of a Hong Kong Community.* The University of Arizona Press, Tucson, 1975.

Papineau, Aristide, J. G., *Hong Kong, a Guide to.* André Publications, Singapore, 1976.

Pope-Hennessy, James, *Half-Crown Colony.* Jonathan Cape, London, 1969.

Rabushka, Alvin, *Value for Money, The Hong Kong Budgetary Process.* Hoover Institution Press, Stanford, 1976.

Savidge, J., ed., *Hong Kong 1976, Report for the Year 1975.* Hong Kong Government Press, Hong Kong, 1976.

Sayer, Geoffrey Robley, *Hong Kong.* Oxford University Press, London, 1937.

Szczepanik, Edward, *The Economic Growth of Hong Kong.* Oxford University Press, London, 1958.

Wiltshire, Trea, *Hong Kong, An Impossible Journey Through History.* Serasia, Hong Kong, 1971.

Wood, Winifred, A., *A Brief History of Hong Kong.* South China Morning Post Limited, Hong Kong, 1940.

Acknowledgements

The author and editors wish to thank the following: Tony Allan, London; Dinshaw and Kiki Balsara, Hong Kong; Norman Bancroft-Hunt, Caterham Hill, Surrey; Jack Braga, Hong Kong; Albert Buenaflora, Hong Kong; Jack Cater, C.B.E., Hong Kong; Francis and Monica Cheung, Hong Kong; Dr. A. W. Dawson-Grove, M.B.E., Hong Kong; Richard C. Clarke, London; Charles Dettmer, Thames Ditton, Surrey; Frank Eckermann, Hong Kong; Harold Ellithorpe, Hong Kong; Hugh Gibb, Hong Kong; Brian Gilmore, Auckland; Susan Goldblatt, London; Bill Henderson, Jardine, Matheson & Co. Ltd., Hong Kong; Hong Kong Government Information Office, London; Hong Kong Government Information Services, Hong Kong; Hong Kong Trade Development Council, Hong Kong and London; Robin Hutcheon, Hong Kong; Hunting Surveys Ltd., London; Yen Kitung, Hong Kong; Christopher Leong, Studio Dinshaw Balsara, Hong Kong; Renate Kohler, London; Kai Yin Lo, Hong Kong; Mr. and Mrs. Lo, Hong Kong; Grace Ma, Hong Kong; Colina MacDougall, London; No. 28 Squadron, Royal Air Force, Hong Kong; Desmond O'Reilley Mayne, Q.C., C.M.G., Hong Kong; Clive Warman, Hong Kong; Lt.-Col. Wilson and 1st Battalion Light Infantry, Hong Kong.

Index

Numerals in italics indicate a photograph or drawing of the subject mentioned.

Colour reproduction by Irwin Photography Ltd., at their Leeds Studio
Filmsetting by C. E. Dawkins (Typesetters) Ltd., London, SE1 1UN.
Printed and bound in Italy by Arnoldo Mondadori, Verona.